DRAMA WITHIN DRAMA

Robert Egan

DRAMA WITHIN DRAMA

SHAKESPEARE'S SENSE OF HIS ART

in *King Lear, The Winter's Tale,*
and *The Tempest*

COLUMBIA UNIVERSITY PRESS
New York and London 1975

822.33

Eg1d

The Andrew W. Mellon Foundation, through a special
grant, has assisted the Press in publishing this volume.

Library of Congress Cataloging in Publication Data

Egan, Robert, 1945–
    Drama within drama.

    Includes bibliographical references.
    1. Shakespeare, William, 1564–1616—Technique.
I. Title.
PR2995.E34   822.3'3   74–20943
ISBN 0–231–03919–0

For my Parents
CHRISTOPHER EDWARD EGAN

and

MARY COLLINS EGAN
with love and gratitude

ACKNOWLEDGMENTS

It may seem surprising that so brief a book should claim so many godparents. Nonetheless, I have received help and encouragement from many quarters, and it is an enjoyable task to recount here my debts of gratitude. For the last few years I have felt the frustration Sebastian expresses in *Twelfth Night:*

> I can no other answer make but thanks,
> And thanks, and ever thanks; and oft good turns
> Are shuffled off with such uncurrent pay.

Whether to be thanked in print is any more "current" a pay than to be thanked in person I do not know, but at least it gives some comfort to the debtor.

Portions of the fourth chapter appeared as an article in *Shakespeare Quarterly,* and I am grateful to Dr. R. J. Schoeck and the Editorial Board of *S.Q.* for permission to reprint them here.

William F. Bernhardt and David Diefendorf of Columbia University Press have guided this book rapidly and sympathetically through publication, dealing patiently with the naiveté of an author new to the process. I am also grateful to Christian S. Ward for his painstaking preparation of the final manuscript and to Columbia University for a grant aiding in the costs of typing.

It has been my good fortune to study Shakespeare in his own school, and much of what insight into the plays I have is owing to my fellow actors and directors at the Marin Shakespeare Festival and the University of New Hampshire Summer Repertory Theatre. In particular, I shall always be indebted to John Edwards, Producing Director of the latter, for casting me as Prospero several years ago. How well I served the ends of his production I cannot say, but properly speaking I began this book then.

At Stanford University, Professor V. A. Kolve supervised a preliminary study that eventually led to this project, and set for me an influential example of dramatic scholarship relevant to theatrical practice. Professors Eleanor Prosser and Ronald Rebholz read this work in its early form as a dissertation, giving it a degree of detailed, constructive scrutiny that continues to amaze me as I attempt to do the same for others. Many of their suggestions are incorporated in the final version.

A number of my colleagues at Columbia University—Professors Robert W. Hanning, S. F. Johnson, George Stade, and Edward W. Tayler—have read this study either as a whole or in part, and I am very grateful for their encouragement and advice. I am grateful, too, to Professor Daniel Javitch for hours of patient listening and helpful commentary at a time when the development of my ideas needed precisely those two aids.

The chief debt I have incurred in writing this work is to my teacher and friend, Professor Virgil K. Whitaker, who has overseen and prompted the work's development through its metamorphoses from article to dissertation to book. His gift for fostering and clarifying strengths on the one hand and, on the other, pinpointing flaws and restraining excesses has exerted a formative influence that I have relied upon throughout. In a very real sense, his concern and persisting interest have made this book possible.

What I owe Marlene Egan pertains to far more than the writing of this book, and I would not attempt to express that debt here. Let it suffice that in this, as in many other matters, I have been deeply fortunate to have the benefit of her advice, support, humor, and exceeding patience.

New York
September, 1974

R. E.

CONTENTS

DRAMA WITHIN DRAMA

Chapter One

INTRODUCTION

I

My aim in this study is to present *King Lear, The Winter's Tale,* and *The Tempest* as a triad representing Shakespeare's concept of his art during the last years of his career. To this end, the following three essays will endeavor to show how Shakespeare has bodied forth the artistic purpose of each play through its characters' attempts to control or alter reality directly through the exercise of dramatic illusion. It is my contention that the success or failure of each such attempt indicates a relationship between the play-world and its inhabitants' artistry that in turn shapes or qualifies the relationship intended by Shakespeare between the art of the play itself and the real world of its audience. In applying this thesis, I hope to elucidate the art of each play through a study of the aesthetic and moral problems of art depicted within that play and so to describe the spectrum of Shakespeare's dramatic self-consciousness in its final phase.

This perspective will, I trust, become fully clear in the application, but a preliminary clarification is in order. The most overt example is afforded by the last of the plays dealt with; and indeed my interests in this area began with a study of *The Tempest*. It is obvious enough that Prospero attempts to deal with his world through explicitly dramatic means and that, moreover, those means are generally quite outside the conventional bounds of a theatrical presentation. Unlike the spectators to an overtly artificial play-within-a-play, those upon whom he works his art are initially quite unaware that what they are witnessing is a fictive spectacle; Prospero directly substitutes his dramatic illusions for reality in their eyes. It is also clear that the motives and results of Prospero's efforts are closely tied to Shakespeare's sense of his own art. No less significant, if less obvious, are attempts by Edgar and Lear in *King Lear* and Camillo and Paulina in *The Winter's Tale* to accomplish similar kinds of dramatic artifice. Not only do these latter attempts effectively define the art of the plays in which they occur, but together they prepare for and contribute to the aesthetic sophistication and scope of *The Tempest*.

Almost whenever it occurs, the portrayal within a play of a direct application of dramatic art to life affords a significant and manifold perspective on both the world of the play and the world surrounding it. The drama of our own century has employed this device frequently and with seemingly endless variations, from Pirandello's *Enrico IV* to Stoppard's *Rosencrantz and Guildenstern Are Dead*. Perhaps the most analogous modern instance for our purposes is Genet's *The Balcony*, which is set in Mme. Irma's bordello, an extraordinary institution whose customers act out, in private theatres and with the aid of prostitute-actresses, the heroic roles that are unavailable to them in real life: mechanics, clerks, and plumbers play at being generals, judges, and bishops. But midway through the play a state of anarchy in the world outside the studios of The Grand Balcony makes it possible for the actor-patrons to go forth, clad in outsize costumes and walking on cothurni, to assume in the real world the identities they have hitherto only acted. Costumed as General, Judge, and Bishop, they take on the actual functions of their roles, led by Madame herself as the Queen. They are quite successful, for the world, they discover, is governed by a universal hunger for illusions, costumes, and roles: a hunger which they, in their purely artificial identities, are ideally suited to fulfill. At the conclusion of the play, Irma, back in her brothel, addresses the audience:

In a little while, I'll have to start all over again . . . put the lights on again
. . . dress up. . . . Dress up . . . ah, the disguises! Distribute roles again
. . . assume my own. . . . Prepare yours . . . judges, generals, bishops,
chamberlains, rebels who allow the revolt to congeal, I'm going to prepare my
costumes and studios for tomorrow. . . . You must now go home, where everything—you can be quite sure—will be falser than here. . . . You must go
home now. You'll leave by the right, through the alley. . . . It's morning already.[1]

The moment is at once fascinating and chilling: just as we have seen
the artifice prevalent in The Grand Balcony move beyond its walls to
encompass and dominate the play-world at large, so the artificial
boundaries of the play itself now open out to subsume and contain our
world. In the process, a comprehensive definition is achieved, not only
of the theatrical event of the play itself, but of the nature of the world
in which that event has occurred.

It is a parallel technique—a similarly significant manipulation of
the play's aesthetic boundaries, internal and external—that we shall
trace through King Lear, The Winter's Tale, and The Tempest. But the
analogy is not a complete one; Shakespeare, though he employs the
same technique, attempts a far fuller definition of his own artwork, en-
courages a more vital response from his audience, and generally works
toward an opposite kind of perspective on both art and experience.
Genet dissolves the distinction between reality and drama in order to
show that the former's standards of meaning and identity are as
ephemeral and false as those of the latter. Shakespeare, quite to the
contrary, deals with an urge to actualize in reality the vital patterns of
order inherent in art. His treatment of whether or not such an urge actually can be fulfilled varies significantly among the plays we shall
regard, but the urge itself remains identifiably constant.

An impulse on the artist's part to order the real world as he orders
his created world no doubt has remained close to the fictive arts of any
age, but there is a particularly lively concern with it implicit in the
aesthetics of Shakespeare's own time. George Puttenham begins his

Arte of English Poesie by laying an enthusiastic stress on the Poet "as a maker. . . . Such as (by way of resemblance and reuerently) we may say of God: who without any trauell to his diuine imagination, made all the world of nought . . . ," and only secondarily on the Aristotelian definition of the Poet as an imitator.[2] Likewise, and far more eloquently, Sir Philip Sidney dwells at length on the Poet's qualities as a maker, a world-creator with a relationship to his creation parallel to that between God and His handiwork, the world itself:

. . . I know not whether by luck or wisedome, we Englishmen have met with the Greekes in calling him a Maker. Which name, how high and incomparable a title it is, I had rather were knowne by marking the scope of the other sciences, then by any partial allegation. There is no art delivered unto mankind that hath not the works of nature as his principall object, without which they could not consist. . . . Onely the Poet disdeining to be tied to any such subjection, lifted up with the vigor of his own invention, doth grow in effect into an other nature: in making things either better than nature bringeth foorth, or quite new . . . so as he goeth hand in hand with nature, not enclosed within the narrow warrant of her gifts, but freely raunging within the Zodiack of his owne wit . . . her world is brasen, the Poets only deliver a golden. . . . Neither let this be jestingly conceived, bicause the works of one be essenciall, the other in imitation or fiction: . . . but so farre substancially it [the process of poetic creation] worketh, not onely to make a Cyrus, which had bene but a particular excellency as nature might have done, but to bestow a Cyrus upon the world to make many Cyrusses, if they will learne aright, why and how that maker made him. Neither let it be deemed to sawcy a comparison, to ballance the highest point of mans wit, with the efficacie of nature: but rather give right honor to the heavenly maker of that maker, who having made man to his owne likenes, set him beyond and over the workes of that second nature, which in nothing he sheweth so much as in Poetry . . .[3]

These terms must have caught Shakespeare's interest; at least they adumbrate the concerns which this study will trace. In particular, the definition of fictive art as the making of a world that is not only independent of and above the world of nature but capable of directly influencing and shaping that world—of "bestowing a Cyrus upon the world to make many Cyrusses"—points to the impulse we are dealing with.[4] Sidney, of course, is speaking figuratively. He does not claim literally that the Poet can create Cyruses and bestow them upon the real world but that, in emulating the imitated ideal of Cyrus held up to them, those in the Poet's audience will themselves grow to be like that image. Yet Sidney's very choice of figurative terms betrays a poet's unrenounced desire for just such direct power to mold the real world. The tension between his literal meaning and his metaphor implies a tension between concepts of the poet as imitator and as mage, a dialectic which to a considerable extent defines, as we shall see, the aesthetic relationship among the three plays we are concerned with.

II

The phase of dramatic self-consciousness represented by *King Lear*, *The Winter's Tale*, and *The Tempest* is not only the last but, I would argue, the fullest of its kind in the Shakespeare canon. There are, of course, frequent depictions of drama within the earlier plays and even, particularly in the disguise plots of the comedies, applications of dramatic illusion to reality. There are as well a number of attempts to relate the world of the play to that of its audience, though these are often veiled by the apologetic stance of an epilogue like Puck's or hinted at and withdrawn as in the final stanza of Feste's song. But nowhere in the canon are the two elements—dramatic art within the play and the dramatic art of the play—so organically joined in a dynamic whole as in these three works. And though in the Sonnets Shakespeare may earlier have presented his lyric art as nature's champion against time, only gradually, throughout the majority of his career, does he develop a sense of his dramatic art as an active force in the world.

We can trace that development, and a correspondingly deepening artistic self-consciousness, through four works that span Shakespeare's early and middle periods. Among the earliest plays we find a surprising application of dramatic artifice to reality as Shakespeare, perhaps embellishing on the work of another dramatist, frames and to a consid-

erable extent defines the drama of *The Taming of the Shrew* by a
lengthy, two-scene Induction. In this sequence, which renders the
whole of *Shrew* as a kind of play-within-a-play, a Lord comes upon
the sleeping drunkard Christopher Sly and, on a sudden whim, con-
structs a manifold fiction around him. He is to be taken to the Lord's
chamber, roused, and convinced that he is a great nobleman: that all
his life as Sly has been but the imagery of a fevered dream. The
awakening of Sly is presented with considerable relish. Along with the
primary joke of Sly's deception and the ease with which he exchanges
his own sense of reality for the illusion enveloping him, we are presented with several reminders of the illusionary powers of art. The
Servants exalt the pleasurable fantasies that pictures can convey (Induction ii, 51–62), and the page Barthol'mew gives an excellent dis-
play of acting ability by masquerading as Sly's wife.[5] Into this maze
of artifice comes a band of players, themselves victims of the Lord's
joke, to play *The Taming of the Shrew* before one who they have been
told is a great lord, and thus the play proper begins.

Not until the three plays we shall deal with does Shakespeare
show a character practicing so complex a fictive art directly upon the
inhabitants of his world. Yet there is a crucial difference between the
Induction to *Shrew* and the artistically reflexive devices of *King Lear,
The Winter's Tale,* and *The Tempest.* Whereas the latter, as I will attempt to show, seriously seek to usher the play's art into the world of
its audience, the *Shrew* Induction merely introduces us to the play as a
pleasurable illusion, and the terms of that introduction imply no claim
to influence or alter our world. The Lord's purposes in weaving his
dramatic fiction around Sly are emphatically unserious. He does not
pretend to change permanently Sly's view of himself or of the world;
indeed, we are assured that Sly will easily make the transition from
illusion back to reality unchanged, dismissing what he has experienced
"even as a flattering dream or worthless fancy" (Induction i, 44). The
very complexity of the situation—the actors playing out their fiction of
Kate and Petruchio within the encompassing fiction of Sly's lord-
ship—only calls attention to the essentially illusory quality of the

drama as a whole. It is all a joke, a harmless, entertaining pastime, and we are invited to share in the fun—to watch the play—with no more profound sentiments than Sly's own: "Come, Madam Wife, sit by my side and let the world slip. We shall ne'er be younger" (Induction ii, 145–147).

Shakespeare further explores the sense of his art as illusion in *A Midsummer Night's Dream*. Here, in the gests of Oberon and Puck, we are forced to recognize the prevalence and power of illusion and fantasy in human experience. If Bottom, Sly's successor, can brush off his temporary metamorphosis as a mere dream, there are others in the play's world who have been permanently altered by their night of "dreaming." Even so, Shakespeare seems reluctant to establish an outright identification between Oberon's powers and those of his own art. Throughout the play, the exploits of the Fairies are counterpointed by the slapstick bumblings of the Mechanicals in their attempt to mount an actual drama. The climax of their efforts comprises the play's culminating scene, which in a self-parodic vein reminds us again and again of how insubstantial and fragile a thing dramatic illusion is. "The best in this kind are but shadows," says Theseus, "and the worst are no worse if imagination amend them" (V.i.214–215). But what Shakespeare chooses to show us in "Pyramus and Thisbe" is how much worse "a tedious brief scene" (56) can be when imagination is lacking in the actors and tolerance in the audience. Here, as in the disastrous pageants of *Love's Labor's Lost,* he seems to be exorcizing through laughter the audience's potential rejection of his own drama. If Puck's epilogue suggests an association between the "weak and idle theme" (434) of Shakespeare's play and the dream visions to which it has lent an aura of significance, that suggestion is heavily muted by the humble context of the speech. The performers, it declares, are indeed "shadows" (430), whose greatest ambition is the "unearnèd luck" (339) of escaping censure. Failing this, they ask only to be dismissed as harmless apparitions.

Thus, whether we are shown its power to entertain or its vulnerability to interruption, drama is emphasized in the earlier plays as something essentially unreal, something which—far from having a direct influence on the world—requires, if it is to exist at all, an audience that is indulgent or drunk enough to "let the world slip" for a time. Not until midway through his career does Shakespeare indicate in his plays a significantly altered sense of his art. This occurs in *Hamlet*, along with the most significant play-within-a-play sequence (the first in the context of a tragedy) up to this point in the canon. The Players come to Elsinore direct from Elizabethan London, bringing with them a wealth of references to such matters as the War of the Theatres, "Hercules and his load," the practical problems of acting, and the unruliness of clowns. In none of his plays does Shakespeare refer in more explicit detail to the practice of his art as a contemporary reality. And amid the tangible atmosphere of excitement and anticipation which the Players' arrival causes, Hamlet ponders the drama as a potential force in his world. After the chief Player's passionate rendition of the Pyrrhus speech (II.ii.490–541), Hamlet launches into the meditation that begins,

> Oh, what a rogue and peasant slave am I!
> Is it not monstrous that this player here,
> But in a fiction, in a dream of passion,
> Could force his soul so to his own conceit
> That from her working all his visage wanned,
> Tears in his eyes, distraction in's aspect,
> A broken voice, and his whole function suiting
> With forms to his conceit? And all for nothing!
> For Hecuba!
> What's Hecuba to him or he to Hecuba,
> That he should weep for her? What would he do
> Had he the motive and the cue for passion
> That I have?
>
> (576–588)

This self-castigating comparison of the Player's art to Hamlet's own situation depends on the concept we have traced above: of drama as groundless illusion, "a fiction . . . a dream of passion" distinct from reality. Yet the very effectiveness of the Player's efforts brings Hamlet to conclude this same soliloquy on quite a different note as regards the uses of dramatic fiction:

> Hum, I have heard
> That guilty creatures sitting at a play
> Have by the very cunning of the scene
> Been struck so to the soul that presently
> They have proclaimed their malefactions;
> For murder, though it have no tongue, will speak
> With most miraculous organ. I'll have these players
> Play something like the murder of my father
> Before my uncle. I'll observe his looks,
> I'll tent him to the quick. If he but blench,
> I know my course.
> .   .   .   .
> The play's the thing
> Wherein I'll catch the conscience of the King.
>   (617–627; 633–634)

Thus for the first time Shakespeare openly treats the concept of drama as an instrument to influence and even shape reality. In having his hero resort to dramatic artistry to purge his corrupt world Shakespeare is no doubt conscious of his predecessor in the revenge genre, Thomas Kyd, who brashly asserted the power of his art in having Hieronymo, hero of *The Spanish Tragedy,* effect his revenge by composing and directing a tragedy with his enemies as actors, arranging for them to be murdered in truth when his script calls for their deaths as characters. In the actual results of Hamlet's artistic project, however, Shakespeare forgoes Kyd's gambit for a sequence that is both more subtle and less conclusive as a reflection on the potentialities of his own drama.

In fact, Hamlet's play does not actually enable him to "know" his "course." It does visibly catch the King's conscience, but the certainty this brings to Hamlet of Claudius' guilt by no means prompts him to an immediate and decisive action. Shortly afterwards, in fact,

he forgoes the opportunity to kill Claudius (on very uncertain terms if
revenge is his only motive) and returns, after the abortive act of mur-
dering Polonius, to his former pattern of alternate rage and brooding
over the problems that have obsessed him from the play's start. For
Hamlet's chief need is not a detective's clue but a new world. His
overriding concern is a dialectic with the very terms of existence; and
while the fact that Hamlet Senior has been murdered and his place
usurped by the murderer has become for Hamlet the chief type of humanity's degradation from an angelic paragon to a quintessence of
dust, the mere exposure and death of Claudius can no more amend the
world Hamlet apprehends than it can cleanse a foul and pestilent
congregation of vapors from the air or restore the earth from a sterile
promontory to a goodly frame.

Hamlet's drama, then, falls short of being the active instrument to
shape the nature of things that he had hoped it would be. Yet it does
prove effective in another way, attaining that same end Hamlet has
told the Players is the purpose of their art:

. . . to hold as 'twere the mirror up to Nature—to show Virtue her own fea-
ture, scorn her own image, and the very age and body of the time his form and
pressure.

(III.ii.24–27)

Indeed, *The Murder of Gonzago* accomplishes this end, reflecting the
nature of the world as Hamlet sees it, a good deal more effectively
than it catches the conscience of the King. The actual murder of the
Player King is noticeably shallow as drama; it is, as Hamlet's impa-
tient comments suggest (III.ii.262–264), little more than melodramatic
cliché. What catches our attention far more is the dialogue of the
Player King and Queen, in particular the King's long discourse on the
evanescence of human purpose and conviction before the relentless,
arbitrary forces of change and circumstance (197–223). Mannered and
rigidly versified as it is, this passage retains a curious effectiveness. It
conveys a symmetrical image of existence as Hamlet views it, reduc-
ing to proverbial form the essence of all his *cris de coeur*—that certain

debilitating conditions are laid on our lives rendering us helpless to define or control what we are:

> Our wills and fates do so contráry run
> That our devices still are overthrown,
> Our thoughts are ours, their ends none of our own.
>
> (221–223)

So succinct a commentary is this on Hamlet's own predicament that one feels it must comprise that "speech of some dozen or sixteen lines" (II.ii.566) that he himself has written.

Mimesis, then, the ability to reflect reality in an effective image that codifies and communicates the artist's vision: this is what Shakespeare defines as the utmost power of drama in *Hamlet*. It is, perhaps, his most realistic assessment of what his art, in its contemporary form, can accomplish in the world as he knows it. As such, this assessment is bounded by the recognition that in its conventional context drama can mirror the world but not directly affect or alter it, and this recognition, as we shall see in *King Lear*, will continue to inform his strictest definitions of the power of his art. Yet even in the final moments of *Hamlet* there is evidence of a frustrated impulse to accomplish more than a mirroring of reality—to establish some direct bridge between the created world of the play and the real world of its audience. Hamlet, in dying, all but explicitly recognizes that he is in the presence of a theatrical audience:

> You that look pale and tremble at this chance,
> That are but mutes or audience to this act,
> Had I but time—as this fell sergeant, Death,
> Is strict in his arrest—oh, I could tell you—
> But let it be.
>
> (V.ii.345–349)

He strives to communicate into our world some message, some sense of the meaning contained in what has befallen him, but Death lowers a curtain of silence. Hamlet does charge Horatio with the task of re-

maining in the world "To tell [Hamlet's] story" (360), but the only
story Horatio can tell is a *résumé* of the play *Hamlet*:

> give order that these bodies
> High on a stage be placèd to the view,
> And let me speak to the yet unknowing world
> How these things came about. So shall you hear
> Of carnal, bloody, and unnatural acts,
> Of accidental judgments, casual slaughters,
> Of deaths put on by cunning and forced cause,
> And, in this upshot, purposes mistook
> Fall'n on the inventors' heads. All this I can
> Truly deliver.
>
> *Fortinbras.*   Let us haste to hear it,
> And call the noblest to the audience.
>
>   (388–398)

The theatrical implications of bodies disposed on a stage before an audience are self-evident, and Horatio's indication of what his explanation to the yet unknowing world will be is precisely a catalogue of the
dramatic events we have witnessed. By way of explicating what has
transpired in the play, Horatio, in effect, convenes an audience for a
repeat performance of that play. Instead of opening out to disclose
some revelation akin to that attempted by Hamlet at the moment of his
death, the play turns back upon its own artificial sphere as the ultimate
explanation of its meaning.

Shakespeare, however, continues his exploration of the impulse
to establish some concrete relationship between the art of his play and
the world of his audience. In the process, he turns from the confining
realism of the play-within-a-play convention, with its overt boundary
between play and reality, towards a more imaginative and flexible
mode: that of portraying the direct application of drama to reality in
such a way as not only to define drama as a dynamic element within
the play's world, but to establish a cognate place for the play itself in
the world of its audience. The most significant uses of this mode
occur, of course, in the plays which the following three essays will

focus upon. We can, however, trace Shakespeare's first substantial ex-
periment in this direction through the denouement of *As You Like It*.
Acting the part of Ganymede, Rosalind employs a considerable
amount of role-playing and improvised drama toward the reshaping
and improvement of her world via the pairing-off of its lovers with
their appropriate mates. The climax of her efforts and of the play itself
is a formal festival attended by all the play's chief characters, to whom
she has promised that she will arrange the appearance of Rosalind, her
wedding with Orlando, and the marriage of every other lover to his
lass. All this she proposes to effect through powers given her by "a
magician most profound in his art and yet not damnable"
(V.ii.66–67). She does bring about such a seemingly miraculous outcome, not by magic *per se* but by a theatrical event: her own ritual unmasking.

This metaphorical association (which Shakespeare will repeat and
elaborate in both *The Winter's Tale* and *The Tempest*) between dramatic art, as Rosalind has practiced it upon her world, and magic, an
art which by definition can control and shape reality, is then applied in
the Epilogue beyond the play's fictional context to the intended relationship between *As You Like It* and its audience. "Rosalind," speaking no longer in character but as the actor who has played Rosalind
("If I were a woman . . ."), addresses the audience in the language
of a magician:

My way is to conjure you, and I'll begin with the women. I charge you, O
women, for the love you bear to men, to like as much of this play as please
you. And I charge you, O men, for the love you bear to women—as I perceive
by your simpering none of you hates them—that between you and the women
the play may please.

                                                                (Epilogue. 11–17)

Just as Rosalind has conjured, in dramatic fashion, the inhabitants of
her world, so the artist who has played Rosalind conjures the audience, suggesting that their response to the play be intimately bound up
with their impulse toward sexual love, the same impulse exhibited by

the play's chief characters. Beneath a comic overtone, in other words, the play implies in its art an influence upon the real world parallel to that of Rosalind's art upon hers. Thus Shakespeare prefigures in a kind of rough sketch the mode of dramatic self-consciousness we shall examine in *King Lear, The Winter's Tale,* and *The Tempest*: a firm welding of artistic and moral concerns within and without the play into a unified apprehension of experience.

III

No study of Shakespeare's dramatic self-consciousness in any of its phases can ignore Anne Righter's *Shakespeare and the Idea of the Play,*[6] which I have found a helpful and highly readable study of what the author terms "the play metaphor"—Shakespeare's meaningful balancing, in comparison or contrast, of the play-world with the real world. In her final two chapters Righter recognizes in the late plays, and particularly in the final Romances, a tendency to withdraw the boundary between drama and reality within the play's world, but she interprets this as a decline in the clarity of Shakespeare's concept of his own art, even as a loss of confidence in the power and significance of drama.[7] I disagree, of course: as this study will make clear, my approach assumes that Shakespeare's withdrawal of the boundary constitutes an ultimate scrutiny of the powers of his art, implying a vigorous confidence in the ability of that art to withstand such an ordeal.

A final word on my method of approach: it will be noticed that, in interpreting and commenting upon these plays, I have often couched my reactions and conclusions in the first person plural. I have done so not because I wish to coerce or cajole the reader into adopting my point of view, but because my chief concern in these essays is to convey accurately what I understand to be each play's intended relationship to its audience at the moment of performance. I have, then, employed what might be termed "the spectatorial 'we' " in order that my sense of that relationship may be more accurately conveyed. I offer the viewpoint of this "we" for the reader to evaluate on his own terms, with the hope that it may amplify the possibilities of his own response to any of these plays as artist, audience, or interpreter. Dramatic criticism can intend no more.

Chapter Two

NATURE'S ABOVE ART: "KING LEAR"

I

To designate the aesthetic purpose of *King Lear* as that of tragedy is a simple enough matter, but to attempt a definition of what version of tragic experience the play sets forth, to specify the nature and intent of its impact upon us, is to encounter perhaps the truest indication of its sheer height and breadth as an artwork: the persistency with which it eludes a satisfying critical classification. We can subscribe easily to Keats's epithets, richly accurate by their very ambiguity, of the "Fierce dispute/Betwixt damnation and impassioned clay," the "deep eternal theme," the "old oak Forest"; but as soon as we attempt to set the terms and determine the outcome of that dispute, or to indicate what specific "Phoenix wings" will raise us once we have been "consumed in the fire," our differences rapidly materialize.[1] In one sense this is as it should be. Our particular responses to tragedy ought to be as varied and personal as our particular responses to life: Edgar exhorts us rightly to "Speak what we feel, not what we ought to say" (V.iii.324).[2] Yet of *King Lear* much of a conflicting nature has been said concerning what we ought to feel.

This diversity is due at least partly to the fact that to an unusual extent *King Lear* either leaves unsatisfied or specifically frustrates the instinctive desire for order in experience that motivates much of our response to drama, as indeed to any aesthetic genre. Drama has its roots in religious ritual, and we come to the theatre with expectations of a unified, affirmative structuring of experience that we do not necessarily find in our daily lives. Not that plays always, or even very often, directly satisfy these expectations by enclosing the events they image in structures of cosmic symmetry and meaning—as do, for instance, the concluding trial in Aeschylus' *Oresteia,* the comedic cycles of the medieval mystery plays, and the realization of the Tudor myth of history in Shakespeare's *Henry VI–Richard III* tetralogy. But any significant theatrical event must in some way recognize such expectations or take them into account. If the universal enigmas and paradoxes that have torn Hamlet are not resolved, they are at least sung to rest, along with the hero, by flights of angels: superseded by a formally Christian conclusion to his pagan mission and agnostic wanderings. Our empathetic involvement with Macbeth is, at the end, balanced by our apprehension of Scotland's purging to a sound and pristine health. And though we have no real explanation for the malevolence of Iago and the susceptibility of Othello, the latter is allowed, to our satisfaction, to pronounce his own eulogy, carry out the State's punishment on himself, and die upon a kiss.

We are, however, afforded markedly little such satisfaction by the final events and denouement of *King Lear.* Lear's own sufferings end, even as they began, in an agony of outcry, confusion, and protest. Moreover, the source of that last agony, the death of Cordelia, is occasioned not by any definably significant cause but by an entirely gratuitous, accidental turn of events—the result finally not of an intentional plan of evil but of bad luck, forgetfulness, and inefficiency. Nor is this the only instance in the play of random mischance with chaotic human results. All the hopes carefully built up by Lear's escape to Dover, the militant return of Cordelia, and her reunion with Lear are shattered in two lines by the offstage, unexplained loss of the battle. All along, in fact, there is an apparent friction between the form of the play and its actual events, which repeatedly seem to rebel against and overrun the boundaries of dramatic convention. Yet it is clear from his reworking of the sources that Shakespeare specifically calculated such an effect. The probable source-play, *The True Chronicle History of King Leir*, ends with a joyous Leir returned to his throne by the victorious Gallia and Cordella, and though Holinshed's version of the story does include the eventual hanging of Cordeilla, she at least dies by her own choice, long after the reinstatement and peaceful death of Leir. In *King Lear*, then, as nowhere else in the Shakespeare canon, our responses as an audience are by design painfully, almost offensively, manhandled in a series of clashing ironies, unexpected and unprepared-for turns of plot, and cruel confrontations with suffering of the kind that discouraged Samuel Johnson from reading the play again without first revising its last scenes.[3]

Dr. Johnson's honest desire to change the play in order to avoid personal discomfort provides a significant type of much critical reaction to *Lear*. The most obvious examples, of course, are the Restoration and eighteenth-century adaptations of the play, notably Nahum Tate's, which attached a happy, poetically just denouement and added a love plot between Cordelia and Edgar to boot.[4] But the *Lear* criticism of our own time has often found subtler ways, if not of altering the text itself, yet of emending our response to it, either by avoiding altogether its chain of haphazard disasters and gratuitous sufferings or by accommodating them exclusively to a glib sense of the absurd. The first extreme is typified by the recent tendency to classify the play as an essentially Christian morality drama or at least a work of orthodox theodicy. This reading—which in part stems from A. C. Bradley's tentative definition of the play as "The Redemption of King Lear"[5]—in taking the central movement of the play to be Lear's progress toward self-knowledge and serenity, inevitably fails to account for the enormity of Cordelia's death and the turbulence of Lear's final agony. Bradley therefore termed the ending dramatically faulty, but later critics have attempted to resolve the problem by stating, as O. J. Campbell does, that "it is not what the earthly Cordelia *is*, but what she *represents* that is important . . . she is hanged, as Christ was crucified, so that mankind might be saved.'' [6] Further, Bradley's debatable suggestion that Lear's last speech expresses the conviction that Cordelia lives [7] has been expanded into what Paul N. Siegel considers a beatific vision of "the angelic radiance he was at last about to attain . . . reunited [with Cordelia] in eternal bliss." [8] Beyond the fact that whatever might be called Lear's redemption occurs before Cordelia's death and that nothing is shown to be accomplished by her "sacrifice," I find such an optimistic reading entirely inconsistent with the pain and desolation that clearly dominate the play's outcome.

But if *King Lear* cannot be defined exclusively in terms of its comic pattern and elements of affirmation, neither can it be validly treated without them; and this has been the tendency of some recent criticism and several productions of the play: to focus exclusively on its elements of chaos, suffering, and disintegration. The most influential example is Jan Kott's essay, "King Lear or Endgame," a provocative illumination of the parallels, which certainly exist, between the characters, relationships, and circumstances of twentieth-century absurdist drama, particularly Samuel Beckett's, and the exposition of absurd suffering in *King Lear*. [9] Significantly, though, while Kott presumes to speak of the play as a whole, he never deals with or touches upon any part of it after Gloucester's false suicide and Lear's mad scene at Dover. He simply abstracts all that is grotesque, painful, and hopeless in the storm and Dover scenes, treating his abstract as the essence of the play. The lopsidedness of this approach is self-evident; yet Kott's essay has directly influenced a number of important productions. [10]

A more balanced study of the absurd in the play is J. Stampfer's "The Catharsis of *King Lear*," which takes into account both Lear's growth in charity and humility, culminating in the reunion with Cordelia, and the unalleviated shock of the ending. If the play is to be taken as an aesthetic unity, Stampfer argues, then we must consider Lear, in his full course of purgation and attainment of near-sainthood, as a "test case," proving that once the social contract is broken no amount of purgative suffering or spiritual refinement can save a man from terrible and total destruction, since that contract is a covenant with an "imbecile universe" that has "no charity, resilience, or harmony," and which no penance can ever mollify.[11] This is an insightful and revealing view, but in implying that the regeneration of Lear is nullified and rendered meaningless by his and Cordelia's ultimate fates Stampfer limits our view of the play no less than does Campbell in pronouncing their deaths negligible in light of the salvation they have achieved. All these critics, and the extremes of *Lear* criticism they exemplify, sacrifice the whole sense of the work to establish a uniform means of response to it. Yet our most basic apprehension of the play will allow us to ignore neither Lear's regeneration and Cordelia's love nor the haphazard circumstances and events that dominate the play's latter scenes. The sense of order posited by the self-awareness and charity which Lear acquires in the storm and by the uncompromising human affirmation of his reunion with Cordelia is rendered all the more important by contrast with the tide of chaos that surrounds and eventually overwhelms it, and it is because we undeniably feel the hope and beauty of this order that the annihilations of Lear and Cordelia strike us with a doubly painful effect.

We are left, then, with an unavoidable ambiguity of response to *King Lear,* a dipole motion between order and chaos, affirmation and absurdity, that is confusing, even agonizing. I submit, however, that this ambiguity has a distinct purpose in the artistic scheme of the play, and that we can understand that purpose without attempting, as have the critics discussed above, to resolve the ambiguity itself. It is toward such an understanding that we will apply, in the following chapter, the central premise of this study: that Shakespeare's artistic purpose is reflected within the play itself through attempts by its characters to deal with, influence, or alter the circumstances of their world directly through exercises of dramatic art. We shall examine the failures and successes of such artistry within *King Lear,* establish their contextual significance in the play, and apply the aesthetic criteria they figure forth toward an overview of the play's intended relationship as a work of art to the real world and to us, its inhabitants. This will lead us to a sense of Shakespeare's own conception of his play's art and thus to an illumination of the torturous complex of responses elicited by *King Lear*.

II

The most overt instance of dramatic artifice in the play, and the best initial example of how the play defines itself from within, occurs in IV.vi., when Edgar instills in the blinded Gloucester the illusion that, in the midst of his suicide attempt, a miracle has befallen him. This sequence not only reflects clearly the central problem with which *King Lear* must come to grips as an artwork but also portrays and examines in Edgar's actions the kind of relationship between artwork and audience which Shakespeare has chosen *not* to establish with the audience of *King Lear*. The event occurs at the end of a six-scene interlude in which Lear himself has been offstage. As in the similar intervals of *Hamlet* and *Macbeth,* Shakespeare absents his hero from the action, detaching us temporarily from involvement in his tragic career, to provide us, before the play's final movement, with a more general perspective on its several strands of plot and meaning. This analytical detachment reaches its peak as, within the dramatic event we are witnessing, another dramatic event begins to take shape: not a play within the play, the events of which both actors and onstage spectators take for granted as illusionary, but an attempt on Edgar's part to substitute dramatic illusion directly for reality.

Significantly, Edgar's audience is blind, but otherwise the means and the medium which Edgar employs are quite similar to those Shakespeare has at his disposal. On a bare and empty stage, Edgar conjures up a vivid scene purely by the powers of gesture and fictive language. We are specifically reminded of these mimetic elements by Shakespeare's emphasis on the fact that Gloucester in reality neither feels nor hears any of the sensations of which Edgar succeeds in convincing him:

Glou. When shall I come to th' top of that same hill?

Edg. You do climb up it now; look how we labour.

Glou. Methinks the ground is even.

Edg.   Horrible steep:
Hark! do you hear the sea?

Glou.   No, truly.

       .   .   .   .

Edg. Come on, sir; here's the place: stand still. How fearful
And dizzy 'tis to cast one's eyes so low!
The crows and choughs that wing the midway air
Show scarce so gross as beetles; half way down
Hangs one that gathers sampire, dreadful trade!
Methinks he seems no bigger than his head.
The fishermen that walk upon the beach
Appear like mice, and yon tall anchoring bark
Diminish'd to her cock, her cock a buoy
Almost too small for sight. The murmuring surge,
That on th' unnumber'd idle pebble chafes
Cannot be heard so high. I'll look no more,
Lest my brain turn, and the deficient sight
Topple down headlong.
                                             (IV.vi.1–4, 11–24)

This is, of course, one of Shakespeare's most powerful descriptive speeches: a wealth of visual detail, complete with a standard of perspective, fills out the receding land and seascapes, and the very "murmuring surge" that "Cannot be heard so high" *is* heard in the assonance of the lines that describe it. In the context of a drama that depends almost exclusively on its own language for scene-setting, the passage is apt momentarily to convince us as it convinces Gloucester. Yet paradoxically we know that even on the play's level of reality this panorama is objectively an untruth, a purely artificial product of Edgar's imagining. We are thus being alienated, in the Brechtian sense, from dramatic illusion and forced to confront the exercise of dramatic artifice itself: to evaluate its powers and weigh the ends toward which it is here employed.

Edgar proceeds to play out a dramatic action in the landscape he has created, moving as an actor through a succession of roles that frame and define a central role of protagonist for Gloucester. First Edgar is a calm and articulate version of Poor Tom who brings Gloucester to within a foot of the cliff's edge and leaves him there; then he is an anonymous country fellow who wakes Gloucester from his faint, informing him that he has fallen perpendicularly over ten mast heights without injury, that "the clearest Gods, who make them honours/Of men's impossibilities" (73–74) have miraculously preserved his life, and that Poor Tom was in reality a disguised fiend. Thus the artificial action over which Edgar presides takes the shape of a dramatic allegory, a morality play with Gloucester as an Everyman or Mankind figure, wavering between fiends who draw him on to despair and a benevolently disposed, divine Power that ultimately intervenes to save him from the sin of self-destruction. Besides doubling as Vice and Chorus, Edgar delivers an appropriate epilogue, exhorting Gloucester henceforth to "Bear free and patient thoughts" (80).

Dramatic artistry with a morally didactic intent is not a mode of action new to Edgar. From the beginning, all his deeds have been based on an unshakeable faith that a just order governs the workings of the universe, that all chaos and suffering are part of a greater moral plan within that order, and that if he patiently endures his afflictions long enough their creative, providential purpose will eventually reveal itself. Like Lear, he has been stripped of his identity and thrust out unaccommodated to "outface/The winds and persecutions of the sky" (II.iii.11–12), but his method of coping with the disorder of the storm has not been to rage, as Lear has, against it, but to meet it with "presented nakedness" (11), to submit entirely and willingly to the suffering inflicted upon him, confident that, having endured the worst that the universe can reasonably subject him to, he will return "to laughter," purged and improved by his ordeal (IV.i.6). His purpose, though, has not been simply to affirm what he believes to be the moral order governing experience but to communicate that order to others, and it is partly for this reason that he has assumed the mask of Poor Tom, the *persona* of a corrupt serving-man of Oswald's stripe, whose life of pride, lust and deceit have brought upon him just retribution from "the sweet face of heaven" (III.iv.89–90). Lear has seen in Poor Tom only "the thing itself . . . a poor, bare, forked animal" (III.iv.109–110), a type of absurdly suffering man, and Gloucester has reacted similarly to Edgar's disguise, which has made him "think a man a worm" (IV.i.33); yet it is clear nonetheless that Edgar's intention has been to endow the physical and mental suffering which he acts out with the appearance of moral meaning, of religious cause and effect. The medieval devils that abound in his ravings imply their opposite, a just God or Gods, and he presents his fictional biography as a cautionary tale to impress upon his hearers an orthodox moral code:

Take heed o' th' foul fiend. Obey thy parents; keep thy word's justice, swear not; commit not with man's sworn spouse; set not thy sweet heart on proud array.   (III.iv.80–83)

So confident is Edgar of an ultimate cosmic order, then, that he is willing to body forth the justice of the heavens by overtly artificial means, and these means take an increasingly dramatic form, culminating in the action we are dealing with. Gloucester, when Edgar encounters him in Act IV, has undergone, in the outrage and raw pain of his blinding, an agony of reasonless suffering in payment for his kindness to Lear. That suffering, which we have been forced to witness, has provided a vivid physical analogue to the chaotic suffering which Lear, in his primarily mental agony, has endured at the hands of man and nature. Gloucester, like Lear, has appealed to a higher moral order for retribution, declaring that he will "see/The winged vengeance overtake such children" (III.vii.64–65). And as Lear cried out to whatever gods loved old men or were themselves old, beseeching them to send down and take his part (II.iv.192–195), so Gloucester, even as his eye is ripped out, has cried,

He that will think to live till he be old
Give me some help! O cruel! O you Gods!
(III.vii.68–69)

But as Lear's appeal was answered by the amoral chaos of wind and rain, Gloucester's has been met by their terrible counterparts in human nature: naked power and bestial cruelty. As a result, Gloucester despairs of any ultimate moral order in the universe—"'As flies to wanton boys, are we to th' Gods;/They kill us for their sport'' (IV.i.36–37)—and resolves to renounce the world and his great afflictions by ending his life. Although *King Lear* takes place in a decidedly pagan milieu, such an act and the state of mind that gives rise to it are clearly sinful by Edgar's proto-Christian standards, and he bends all his art, as embodied in the drama of the prevented suicide, toward restoring to Gloucester a faith in the beneficence of the Gods and the patience to submit to their will. In this he is entirely successful. Having experienced Edgar's dramatic image of an ordered universe in which the clearest Gods intervene to rescue men from infernal agents of evil, Gloucester wholly accepts (for the present) Edgar's faith that affliction and chaos, being parts of a divine scheme, will, if borne patiently, cry " 'Enough, enough' and die" (IV.vi.77).

Through an exercise of dramatic art, then, Edgar has reconciled Gloucester to his existence, providing him by illusion with a grounds of belief, a moral and metaphysical means of structuring his experience, which reality has not afforded him. This is, of course, the same end toward which our own theatrical expectations instinctively lean; we would like to come away from our experience of *King Lear* just as Gloucester has come away from the dramatic image Edgar has created for him, with confidence that all experience, suffering included, is contained within a greater plan of cosmic order. Both before and after Shakespeare the Lear fable has been used to satisfy just such expectations. But they are the very expectations which, as we have noted, *King Lear* will not only fail to satisfy but specifically frustrate.

Clearly, then, in Edgar's artistry Shakespeare is providing us with an example of the aesthetic alternative he has chosen not to follow, and the grounds for his choice emerge to a considerable extent through the manner in which that alternative is here portrayed. For our response to Edgar's work of drama is by no means a satisfied or comfortable one. We are never allowed to forget that the entire project rests on the deception and manipulation of a blindman and the substitution of illusory falsehood for experiential truth. The physical agony and metaphysical chaos that have driven Gloucester to a resolution of suicide are real, while the miracle that seems to furnish evidence of the divine presence and concern for which he has cried out in vain is patently an illusion. Further, the manner of the action itself heightens and underlines our uneasiness. There is a certain pagan rightness and finality about what Gloucester supposes to be his death speech (IV.vi.34–40): a gentle but firm nay-saying to the limitless and reasonless affliction which he conceives to be the ''great opposeless wills'' of the Gods.[12] Consequently, the moment when he falls forward and faints is one of terrible anticlimax, far more so in performance than in the text, and nearly as painful to witness, in its profound indignity, as was his blinding. Edgar himself acknowledges this by attempting a defensive explanation of his action. ''Why I do trifle thus with his despair/Is done to cure it'' (33–34); but this does not ameliorate our discomfort. Gloucester may be saved from despair— temporarily at least—but the fact remains that Edgar has shown the heavens just only by a piece of stage trickery; and in doing so he has compromised both Gloucester's integrity and his own truthfulness.[13]

These misgivings are confirmed as, immediately after its epilogue, Edgar's affirmative, morally ordered image of existence is confronted with and discredited by the thing itself—the direct human evidence of the disordered reality which his dramatic art has sought to exclude from its scope of vision. ''Bear free and patient thoughts,'' Edgar concludes, ''But who comes here?'' (80). It is King Lear— Gloucester's greater counterpart in agony—who comes, mad and raging, to recount the play's broadest and most unmitigated vision of universal chaos. What follows is a cracked and crazed mosaic of all the disorder and suffering Lear has endured and witnessed throughout the play. He begins by announcing, ''I am the king himself'' (84), implying in that title all he has discovered as a protagonist representative of all men; for in struggling through the storm to retain the name and the addition of a king, he has attained an entire and mercilessly clear awareness of the identity and integrity afforded to man by nature and the apparent universe at large. He began secure in the conceit that he was "every thing" (107), the archetype of a humanity firmly fixed at the hub of an anthropocentric universe, but that was "no good divinity" (102). For when he exposed himself to the Hobbesian logic of nature and the ambiguous turmoil of the heavens, "When the rain came to wet me once and the wind to make me chatter, when the thunder would not peace at my bidding" (102–104), he found no clearest Gods who make them honors of men's impossibilities but only eyeless, raging elements that tore his white hairs and made nothing of them. To be a man, he has discovered, is to be a creature whose inherent, unaccommodated lot is helpless vulnerability to affliction, a creature whose alternatives are either brute suffering or brutal competition to avoid that suffering. The bestiality that is thus imposed upon and infused with human existence now possesses Lear's mind and erupts in a terrifying fit of disgust with all living flesh, culminating in an emblem that directly recalls and parodies the orthodox, vertically ordered universe imaged by Edgar's drama, with man hovering between clearest Gods and infernal fiends. Lear visualizes Heaven and Hell as the trunk and genitals of the female body, and it is Hell that monopolizes his ravaged consciousness:

> But to the girdle do the Gods inherit,
> Beneath is all the fiend's: there's hell, there's darkness,
> There is the sulphurous pit—burning, scalding,
> Stench, consumption, fie, fie, fie! pah, pah!
>
> (128–131)

Lear goes on to depict a universal panorama of injustice and exploitation, after which, suddenly recognizing the weeping Gloucester, he reaches out in an attempt to comfort him:

> If thou wilt weep my fortunes, take my eyes;
> I know thee well enough; thy name is Gloucester;

Thou must be patient; we came crying hither;
Thou know'st the first time that we smell the air
We wawl and cry.

(178–182)

Again, there is a deliberate and contradictory echo of Edgar's rhetoric. Lear, too, counsels patience to Gloucester, but not because it is demanded and will be rewarded by the Gods—rather because we can expect no alternative to the pain and grief we know, since suffering is synonomous with living: when we begin to live we begin to cry.

This is Lear's vision, culled from his own experience, of "how this world goes" (149). It implies no order, provides recourse to no structures of faith or reason, but it has cut Lear to the brains; and its painful authenticity, positioned as it is beside Edgar's carefully constructed artwork, violently undercuts the latter's ordered illusion of existence. Moreover, Lear's mad aria is marked at its start and finish by reflections upon Edgar's dramatic artistry which, if they are unconscious on Lear's part, cannot be unintentional on Shakespeare's. When Edgar himself exclaims in shock at the entrance of Lear, "O thou side-piercing sight!" (85), Lear responds, "Nature's above art in that respect" (86). He may be continuing his parodic discourse on his own kingship, but his words unavoidably underline the dialectical meaning of his own presence and visual appearance vis-à-vis the form and purpose of the art Edgar has practised. He is decked out in wildflowers, presenting an appropriate icon of man in his natural condition; and we recall Cordelia's description of those flowers:

rank fumiter and furrow weeds,
With hardocks, hemlock, nettles, cuckoo flowers,
Darnel and all the idle weeds that grow
In our sustaining corn.

(IV.iv.3–6)

All are weeds, natural life forms that exist by preying upon and destroying the creatures that sustain and give them life. In this they are

as natural as the cuckoo of the Fool's parable (I.iv.224–225), who
bites off the head that feeds it, or as the pelican to which Lear has referred (III.iv.75), who drinks the heart's blood of its parent—natural,
in short, as the motivations and actions of Goneril, Regan, and Edmund in casting out Lear and blinding Gloucester. This is the nature
Lear has encountered alike in the houses of men and on the open
heath, the atavistic, amoral nature in which man's physical condition
is rooted. Edgar's artificial image of existence has entirely avoided this
datum of human experience, and nature's above art in that respect:
Edgar's art cannot cope with or coexist in the visible presence of the
chaotic nature it has failed to confront. In contrast, Lear, shortly
before leaving the stage, posits his own dramatic image of existence:

> When we are born, we cry that we are come
> To this great stage of fools.
>
> (184–185)

If our lives can be formalized in art, then our parts are those of fools—
sad fools like Lear's own—who wander, singing for sorrow, across
this great stage with only the knowledge that we came crying hither,
that the candle has gone out and we are left darkling. This, Lear
implies, is the only stage image that can contain the chaotic vision of
the world his agony has afforded him.

Moments later Cordelia's soldiers find Lear, Oswald fights with
and is killed by Edgar, and Goneril's plan to murder Albany is uncovered. In short, the plot resumes its rapid momentum and enters its
final phase. But out of this static interlude on the fields of Dover, de-
tached from the play's proper flow of events, has emerged a kind of
apologia for the art of the play *King Lear*. Shakespeare has shown us
in Edgar's artistry a drama that superimposes a scheme of order and
meaning upon experience by entirely artificial and illusory means. We
have seen that such an artistry rests on an essentially deceptive and
manipulative relationship between artist and audience, and the inter-
vention of Lear has shown that the aesthetic product of such an art
cannot remain valid in the face of the reality it has ignored: its image

of existence shatters when held up to nature. Thus we are provided
with a perspective on the dramatic images of the play to come: *King
Lear* is a work of art that undertakes to cope with the worst in human
experience, and if only to validate whatever possibilities of order it
may set forth, it will maintain a stark and unflinching view of the cosmic disorder that hangs over all. To alleviate this in any way would be
to compromise the whole vision of the work and delude its audience,
just as Edgar has compromised himself and deluded Gloucester.
Rather, *King Lear* must establish an image of existence that will remain valid in the face of the darkest realities of experience.

III

Yet how can an artwork that attempts to bring any sense of order to
bear on an inherently chaotic reality hope to survive the gap between
illusion and reality that has discredited Edgar's drama? Lear has implied that the only dramatic image of existence that can do so is one
which, like his great stage of fools, acknowledges the entire absence
of order, direction, or even hope. But Lear's part in the dialectic we
have here examined is only one stage in his own continuing struggle
throughout the play to confront the chaos of existence directly and to
derive from it some sense of order; and this effort has increasingly
taken on aspects of an artistic and finally a dramatic form. Thus the
agony that has impelled Lear to interrupt Edgar's drama reflects in its
own way upon the artistic intent of the play itself. Not only does it
adumbrate the aesthetic problem which Edgar's effort confirms, but,
more important, it prefigures the means with which Shakespeare will
eventually confront that same problem in the play's denouement. Let
us, then, trace the development and significance of Lear's artistry
before proceeding to treat how, in unison with Edgar's, it qualifies and
shapes the artistry of the play itself.

Much of the present century's criticism has seriously diminished
our image of Lear by focusing almost exclusively on what happens to

him rather than on what he does and attempts to do. Whether he is regarded as a wayward sinner who is humbled, taught to repent and saved, or as a victim who is absurdly "hunted down, driven insane, and killed by the most agonizing extremes of passion," [14] the emphasis always falls on passive verbs. This may be due in part to the fact that Lear's tragic agon occurs far less on a plane of physical action than on one of metaphysical apprehension. Yet on the latter level he confronts, challenges, and attempts to rectify all the forms of disorder, general and particular, that apply to the suffering condition of humanity: the bestial, predatory tendency in man himself, the amoral and viciously competitive pattern of nature, and the haphazardness and apparent indifference of the universe at large. The assumption, by so astute a critic of the play as John Danby, that "Lear in his madness cannot feel . . . is spared the real suffering of remorse or the real agony of compassion," [15] is not only false to the actual nature of insanity but directly counter to the essence of Lear's madness, which is a very excess of awareness. His "high rage," (II.iv.298) as Gloucester terms it, is the sacred frenzy of a seer locked in confrontation with the most chaotic truths of experience. Within a world image that bodies forth our most pessimistic fears about the nature of our existence, we are presented in Lear with a hero who, fully encountering the chaos of that existence, eloquently and unceasingly voices our protest against it.

This agonistic sense of his tragedy, and the attendant aspects of artistry with which we are here concerned, do not properly begin until the third act, when Lear rushes out into the storm. Up to that point, *King Lear* is more a drama of education than of agony. Lear begins the play firmly in the grip of an egocentric illusion of universal order: as the King, the chiefest of men, he is imperiously confident of his identity as the unquestioned authority over his subjects, the beloved father of his children, the lord over nature and the appointed deputy of the Gods. All those around him he judges and evaluates only as they conform to his will and satisfy his whims. Therefore, when Cordelia offers him love only according to her bond, refusing to compromise her own integrity by participating in the lavish public contest which he has arranged—a selfish exchange in which love is weighed and priced as a saleable commodity—he unhesitatingly expels her from his world on the principle that "Nothing will come of nothing" (I.i.90): if she cannot gratify his appetite then she is a "little-seeming substance" (198), valueless as a human being. Better she had not been born than not to have pleased him better. Within this perversely selfish standard of order he relies confidently on the authority of all the deities and powers whom he conceives to be the governors of the universe: in casting out his child he presumes to act "by Apollo" (159), "by Jupiter" (178), and

> by the sacred radiance of the sun,
> The mysteries of Hecate and the night,
> By all the operation of the orbs
> From whom we do exist and cease to be.
>   (109–112)

It is clear to us from the outset that Lear's initial concept of cosmic order is not only mistaken but irresponsible and disastrously immoral. Yet he does not long remain alien to our empathy. We know immediately that he is doomed to painful disillusionment by his assumption that his identity as king, father, and man, being fixed in the macrocosmic scheme of things, must remain unshaken without its worldly supports. But it is the very process of his disillusionment that allows us to identify so entirely with Lear. Modern psychology tells us that we have no ability, at the moment of birth, to distinguish between ourselves and the phenomena of the world around us. We expect the same egocentric universe that we knew in the womb, where all existed only to sustain us and satisfy our needs. But from birth onwards our lives are a progressive and bitter awakening to a universe that is largely alien, often indifferent, and at times antipathetic to what we need and what we conceive ourselves to be. Lear reenacts this same awakening in a matter of days. There is some truth to Goneril's sneer that "Old fools are babes again" (I.iii.20), for Lear, in his age, leaves the womb of his pampered and protected social station to encounter the realities of existence anew, naked and unaccommodated as the least of his subjects. The thoroughness and violence of that encounter invest him with the authority to suffer and speak for all of us; he discovers before our eyes the causes for which we cry when we are born.

Lear's education to the chaotic truths of his world, then, is quickly accomplished. The society that his abdication has created, operating by the same selfish logic which he has applied to Cordelia, reduces him rapidly from the everything he has supposed himself to be to nothing, "an O without a figure" (I.iv.200–201), as the Fool puts it. Nothing will come of nothing, and since he has no power or possessions left to barter with, he is of little value to Goneril and Regan, who accordingly haggle down his worth as an individual from one hundred to fifty to twenty-five to zero (II.iv.233–265). Lear recognizes that, by such an atavistic logic, the inherent worth of naked humanity must be "cheap as beast's" (269), that unaccommodated man has no value and no right to live other than that which nature affords him: a beast's haphazard chance for survival. Lear refuses to accept such terms. He insists that as a man he has a "true need" (272), an identity and worth quite apart from his ability to defend himself and exploit others, and in a just universe he is entitled to that need. Accordingly, he leaves the microcosm of society and takes his case directly to the macrocosm. He enters into dialogue with the Gods themselves, on whose authority and patronage he has relied all along, demanding that they make their order known in the world by avenging his wrongs and reaffirming his identity. But the response he encounters is summarized by the Gentleman:

> his white hair,
> . . . the impetuous blasts, with eyeless rage,
> Catch in their fury, and make nothing of.
> (III.i.7–9)

The lesser chaos of society is enclosed by the greater chaos of the heavens themselves. Evidence of the anthropomorphic deities to whom Lear has cried out is ominously absent. No consciousness directs the elemental turmoil of the impetuous blasts: they are eyeless, their fury having no reasonable direction or purpose. They operate, like Lear's human afflictors, only by nature's relentless, amoral logic of competition for survival and dominance, and by that logic they make nothing of the unaccommodated Lear, confirming on a macrocosmic level the judgment of an amoral society.

Stripped of his secure delusions, then, and naked alike to the fury of nature and the enmity of man (an enmity which only reflects on a multiple human scale his own original ethic of self-gratification), Lear experiences existence on its darkest terms as all men at some point experience it: a turbulent continuum of threatening, disparate phenomena. And as all men must, he sets out to reduce that experience to some bearable and comprehensible scheme of order. Thus begins his agon proper, and we, the gathered community of the audience, ritually assist at the struggle; for Lear's sense of personal outrage will broaden into a general rage for order on behalf of all his kind. Each of his attempts to order the chaotic data of experience, to find out or forge a frame of cosmic meaning that will ratify his human identity, will be informed with a progressively greater awareness of the suffering humanity of whom he is a type, and Lear will thus grow in moral vision as his struggle grows in urgency.

From its start, moreover, that struggle will take a form that is inherently artistic. The urge to order experience is quintessential to all art, and Lear will find in his own conceptual and imaginative powers a means of developing and realizing his ideas of order in a way that the bare facts of experience alone do not afford him. Thus as he grows in moral vision the aesthetic terms in which he couches that vision will likewise increase in sophistication. To borrow Wallace Stevens' phrasing, his "rage for order" will become increasingly a "maker's rage," culminating in an exercise of overtly dramatic art.[16]

The rough beginnings of Lear's fictive urge are discernible in his opening storm speeches:

> Blow, winds, and crack your cheeks! rage! blow!
> You cataracts and hurricanoes, spout

Till you have drench'd our steeples, drown'd the cocks!
You sulph'rous and thought-executing fires,
Vaunt couriers of oak-cleaving thunderbolts,
Singe my white head! And thou, all-shaking thunder,
Strike flat the thick rotundity o' th' world!
Crack Nature's moulds, all germens spill at once
That makes ingrateful man!

(III.ii. 1–9)

Lear is here still possessed of his former delusion that his own suffering is a singular and enormous outrage against the order of the universe, and that the Gods stand ready to punish his daughters with "all the stor'd vengeances of Heaven" (II.iv.163). Yet his senses make it clear enough to him that the storm is falling on his own white head and not those of his daughters. Therefore, he erects a fictional structure of ordered meaning around the chaotic reality of the storm, assuming that the wind, rain, thunder, and lightning that afflict him are indeed the instruments of the wrathful Gods. The elements are "thought-executing," not "impetuous" and "eyeless," as the Gentleman has earlier termed them (III.i.8). Goneril's and Regan's sin against Lear has provoked so great an anger in the Gods that they have resolved, upon Lear's demand for revenge, to destroy the entire human race, to crack the very moulds that could give rise to such ingratitude in man. Accordingly, Lear asserts, he must perish in his own vindication. In this way he temporarily orders and copes with the data of reality. By confronting his experience within a fictional context of his own imagining, he can momentarily feel in control of that experience, even convincing himself, as the imperative mode of his speech indicates, that he presides over the ongoing phenomena of reality: the winds blow and the cataracts spout because he, King Lear, orders them to do so; by Lear's own command the lightning singes his head and thunder strikes the world flat.

By an act of imagination and the power of language, then, Lear can reconcile himself briefly to the circumstances of reality. However, both his artificial vision and the egocentric, vengeful principle of order that informs it are too illusionary and patently removed from the facts

of reality to endure. Lear's attempts to maintain the order of his vision
grow increasingly confused as that order crumbles before the ongoing,
objective reality of the storm's disorder:

> Rumble thy bellyful! Spit, fire! spout, rain!
> Nor rain, wind, thunder, fire are my daughters:
> I tax you not, you elements, with unkindness;
> I never gave you kingdom, call'd you children,
> You owe me no subscription: then let fall
> Your horrible pleasure; here I stand, your slave,
> A poor, infirm, weak, and despis'd old man.
> But yet I call you servile ministers
> That will with two pernicious daughters join
> Your high-engender'd battles 'gainst a head
> So old and white as this. O, ho! 'tis foul.
>
> (III.ii.14–24)

While he begins in the same commanding vein that dominated his
previous speech, his mind reels back to the facts of his true plight: that
he is suffering at the horrible pleasures of man and nature, confirmed
by both as a little-seeming substance—a poor, infirm, weak and de-
spised old man. This realization first cracks and then shatters the artificial image he has created of the storm. At first he attempts to grant
the elements license for their hostility toward him on the basis that
they, unlike his daughters, owe him no kindness. But the fact remains
that he is being equally victimized by storm and daughters alike, and
his one final attempt to give this chaotic fact some comprehensible
form and motive—by envisioning the storm as the "high-engender'd"
action of supreme but capricious beings who have sided with his
daughters—trails off in a despairing cry. Exhausted and frustrated in
this effort to forge an order out of disorder through the manipulation of
fictive language, he resolves to give over the struggle, to "say nothing" (39). But this is only the first of several such episodes in Lear's
agon. He will return to the struggle repeatedly, and the insights which
each attempt affords him will remain to inform the next, gathering to a
cumulative apprehension of moral order and aesthetic possibility.

Lear's next attempt, though it occurs only a few lines later, shows a considerable advance in moral awareness:

> Let the great Gods,
> That keep this dreadful pudder o'er our heads,
> Find out their enemies now. Tremble, thou wretch,
> That hast within thee undivulged crimes,
> Unwhipp'd of Justice; hide thee, thou bloody hand,
> Thou perjur'd, and thou simular of virtue
> That art incestuous; caitiff, to pieces shake,
> That under covert and convenient seeming
> Has practis'd on man's life; close pent-up guilts,
> Rive your concealing continents, and cry
> These dreadful summoners grace. I am a man
> More sinn'd against than sinning.
>
> (49–59)

Once again he turns to the Gods for a sense of universal order. What he seeks at their hands, however, is no longer revenge but justice. Accordingly, he envisions in the storm the image of an actual court of law presided over by the great Gods themselves, and the purpose of that court is not only particular justice for Lear but universal justice for humanity. Lear recognizes, now, that there are other crimes committed in his world than ingratitude and other victims of crime than himself: each evildoer who has gone unwhipped of Justice in the social order is now brought before the dreadful summoners of a divine order. Lastly, Lear himself comes to the bar, and his proclamation of the injustice of his own condition has a vitally double-edged quality. Not only does he complain that he has been the victim of sin, but he confesses that he himself has sinned—that he has, implicitly, been an agent of the same amoral and exploitative ethic by which he is now persecuted. Thus Lear seeks in the imaginary court an ultimate source of order that will not only redress the wrongs he suffers but judge and purge the wrongs he has committed.

Just as this vision is informed with a greater moral awareness than the last, so the aesthetic means by which it is achieved involve a more self-conscious, and therefore more effective, exercise of fiction. The speech does not, as do the preceding two, begin in the imperative mood but in the hortative (*"Let* the great Gods . . ."): Lear does not directly command the Gods to find out their enemies as he commanded the wind to blow and the thunder to strike; rather he expresses a wish that they do so and goes on to image the fulfillment of that wish. Instead of attempting to substitute his illusions directly for reality, Lear consciously removes his point of view from the context of reality to that of his own imagination. This allows him an artist's freedom to range freely "within the Zodiack of his owne wit," [17] presiding more efficaciously and uninhibitedly over the ordering of his experience. He can with confidence muster the divine assizes and hale before them each type of human malevolence, building toward his own climactic utterance with a purposeful and unfaltering rhetoric, since his endeavors are now confined not by the bounds of literal fact but by the limits of his own imaginative art.

Yet even this artificial vision cannot survive indefinitely in the presence of the disordered phenomena which it attempts to image. No divine justice is forthcoming from the storm, which remains what it has been all along: an alien and chaotic turmoil of thunder, lightning, wind, and rain. Once more Lear's artificial construct of experience is intruded upon and dispersed by the facts of experiential reality itself. Exhausted again, he is temporarily persuaded by Kent and the Fool to acknowledge that unalterable reality—to "make content with his fortunes fit / Though the rain it raineth every day" (76–77).

But along with this turning of his wits comes a new and major realization. Lear's implied awareness, in his poem of the divine assizes, that the universe contains other victims besides himself grows into the concrete perception that he is not alone in his suffering: "Come on, my boy. How dost, my boy? Art cold? / I am cold myself" (68–69). Thus, for the first time in the play, he experiences compassion, the sharing of suffering. This is an important moment; there is almost certainly a stage image of reaching out and touching between Lear and the Fool—a tentative and protective physical contact as Lear learns,

through the medium of common suffering, to recognize and affirm the
worth of another human being. Such is his first genuine act of love,
and he finds in it a strengthened sense of self—the first scrap of the
identity he has been seeking in a macrocosmic frame of order:

> Poor Fool and knave, I have one part in my heart
> That's sorry yet for thee.
>
> (72–73)

When we next encounter Lear he has expanded this moral insight
into a new, burgeoning vision of order. After another wave of confusion clears, he resolves to "pray" (III.iv.27). His prayer, however, is
significantly not addressed to high-judging Jove, the Goddess Nature,
Hecate, Apollo, or any of the other great Gods to whom he has hitherto appealed for a manifestation of universal order and a ratification
of his own identity. In place of the Gods he directs his religious utterance to all human beings who are his fellow-sufferers:

> Poor naked wretches, whereso'er you are,
> That bide the pelting of this piteous storm,
> How shall your houseless heads and unfed sides,
> Your loop'd and window'd raggedness, defend you
> From seasons such as these? O! I have ta'en
> Too little care of this. Take physic, Pomp;
> Expose thyself to feel what wretches feel,
> That thou mayst shake the superflux to them,
> And show the Heavens more just.
>
> (28–36)

His compassion for the Fool has broadened into an awareness of all
those who have been condemned by man and nature to continual, pur-
poseless, and unjust suffering. He has taken too little care of this, a
condition of existence that operated long before he abdicated his
crown; for his own suffering is not an outrage against the order of the
universe but an instance of a universal reality. This insight carries with
it a terrible import which Lear has not yet fully grasped, but mean-

while it avails him of a new sense of affirmation. By recognizing his kinship with and responsibility for all his suffering kind, he can experience on a general level the love he has found in his heart for the Fool; and this makes possible the object of his prayer, a hopeful sketch of order in the universe. The Heavens have not shown themselves just, but if men (particularly men of power and pomp) could recognize the needs of their fellows, take an empathetic part in their sufferings and minister to their wants, a new fabric of order might be founded on the bonds between man and man instead of those between man and god— bonds of love, of the very kind that have linked Cordelia and France, Kent and Lear, Lear and the Fool, and of the kind which Lear originally broke in casting out Cordelia. Such an order might provide what Lear has sought in his high rage: justice and a means of maintaining the identity and inherent worth of an individual human being.

This concept of a moral order based on human love is a discovery of watershed importance, for it will henceforth inform not only Lear's attempt to order existence but that of the play itself. Lear's mode of speech is here notably less fictive than in the previous lines we have dealt with, since his apprehension of order is now rooted in an actual experience. Yet he does assume, with this apprehension, a sense of aesthetic responsibility that implies and furthers the artistic means by which he has hitherto attempted to envision order. He resolves not only to amend actively the sufferings of his fellows by shaking the superflux to them, but to found upon the moral and physical reality of his actions an image that will *"show* the Heavens more just" (italics mine), furnish suffering humanity with a vision of universal order that the heavenly turmoil of the storm has not revealed. Thus, morally and artistically, Lear directs his struggle for order toward the service of the human community at large. He has accomplished his prayer and he turns to sleep.

But it will be long before Lear is allowed to sleep. This dream of realized order, too, is destined to be overwhelmed by the disorder of reality, as the very insight which has provided Lear with an affirmative view of his own agony presently doubles the dimension and impact of that agony. He has committed himself to feel the sufferings of poor naked wretches whom he has seen only in his mind's eye. Immediately afterward, however, he is confronted with the grotesque incarnation of suffering humanity: Poor Tom,

> the basest and most poorest shape
> That ever penury, in contempt of man,
> Brought near to beast.
>
> (II.iii.7–9)

That Poor Tom is actually Edgar makes him no less "the thing itself" (III.iv.109) that Lear takes him for, a truthful image of afflicted man. Real thorns are impaled in his flesh, real filth grimes his face, and his shivering is unfeigned. He presents not only a reflection of Lear's plight, but a shattering evidence of that plight's universality; the bestial condition to which penury has reduced Poor Tom seems to confirm the one assumption that Lear has striven all along to disprove, that without worldly means of accommodation the life of man is cheap as beast's. The shock of this confrontation shatters Lear's mood of hope and affirmation, plunging him into a nihilistic declaration (103–112) that implies an entire surrender to the chaos of existence: unaccommodated man, he concludes, is no more than a "poor, bare, fork'd animal," who would do better to be in a grave, to be literally nothing, than to attempt to go on living.

Yet Lear's heroic energy and endurance will not let him rest with this despairing acceptance of disorder. Once again, before his long absence from the stage, he resumes his high rage and returns to contest artistically and morally with chaos. This next attempt to order experience, carrying as it does the integrated knowledge of all his previous discoveries, is his most substantial and significant so far in the play. It emerges in III.vi., as Lear's voice rises above the din of Edgar's gibbering, the Fool's eldritch proverbs, and his own frantic hallucinations of revenge to a new clarity of statement and purpose: "It shall be done; I will arraign them straight" (20). In the action that follows he again images the rectification of suffering through the justice of a court of law. Now, however, the justicers he appoints are not the Gods but his fellow men. The defendants are Goneril and Regan, but the issue, besides the particular wrongs they have done to Lear, implies the universal amorality and inhumanity, including Lear's own, which their actions have typified; for Lear now commissions as cojusticers Edgar, Kent, and the Fool, the unaccommodated men who have hitherto suffered most, besides himself, by human cruelty and injustice. It is to this "honorable assembly" (48) of fellow sufferers, representatives of the community of poor, naked wretches to whom Lear dedicated himself in his prayer, that he now pleads his case. The "she-foxes" (23) who preside over society are brought to bay and judged according to a moral code that condemns the sub-human logic by which they and their kind have acted, a code devised and administered by the humanity whom that logic has victimized.

This vision, then, is informed with Lear's greatest moral insight, the concept of an order rooted in human love and circumscribing a compassionate, humane community. Similarly, the aesthetic means, his most sophisticated so far, by which Lear bodies forth this image of order derive their integrity as well from the communal human awareness he has attained. For the fiction over whose creation Lear here presides is not, like his previous visions, a private attempt to wield his experience into an orderly aesthetic pattern; it depends for its fulfillment not merely on Lear's own imagination and utterance but on those of a gathered, ritually participating community as well. Specific roles are formally assigned to be acted out:

> I'll see their trial first. Bring in their evidence.
> [*To Edgar.*] Thou robed man of justice take thy place;
> [*To the Fool.*] And thou, his yoke-fellow of equity,
> Bench by his side. [*To Kent.*] You are o' th' commission,
> Sit you too.
>
>   (36–40)

Thus, as the actors take their places and the trial begins, Lear unmistakably arranges and directs an improvised work of drama. The action that follows has a great deal more impact and focus on stage than its brief appearance in the text alone indicates. Its sudden formality is startling, comic, and yet strangely relieving. For Lear and his companions make full use of the effectively balanced relationship between illusion and reality that drama affords them. The defendants of their play-trial are overtly unreal; they are represented by two joint stools. None of the actor-justicers actually believes that Goneril and Regan are physically present, as their wry joke, depending for its humor on the acknowledged gap between symbol and fact, makes clear:

> *Fool.* Come hither, mistress. Is your name Goneril?
>
> *Lear.* She cannot deny it.
>
> *Fool.* Cry you mercy, I took you for a joint-stool.
>
> *Lear.* And here's another, whose warp'd looks proclaim
> What store her heart is made on.
>
> (50–54)

Yet the community that judges the defendants *is* real, as is the judgment which the dramatic condition of serious play allows them to confer. Lear and his micro-society of sufferers thus effect an imitative rite which, while it does nothing in fact to eliminate the evil of Goneril and Regan from their world, yet manages briefly to exorcise that evil from their collective consciousness. For a moment, a true moral need is thus expressed and fulfilled through dramatic artifice.

Nevertheless, as the vein of self-conscious artificiality in which this dramatic action is performed implies, the chaotic forces and factors with which it comes to grips in art remain quite unaffected in reality. For all the moral awareness and aesthetic vitality with which it is charged, the play-trial cannot actually deprive Goneril and Regan of their political power; as Gloucester's blinding in the following scene will make clear, the she-foxes can manipulate law and violate justice at their own horrible pleasures. Further, art can in no way alter the primal conditions of existence that have given rise to such human bestiality. Lear's question, ''Is there any cause in nature that make these hard hearts?'' (78–79) is rhetorical; by now his experience has provided him with a manifestly affirmative answer.

But Lear's response to this reality is a unique one. Up to now, each of his imaginative visions of order has been foiled and dispersed by an external intrusion of the disordered reality (the continued turmoil of the storm or the sudden appearance of Poor Tom) which that vision has sought to enclose or explain. Now, however, Lear does not wait for such an intrusion. Recognizing that this artificial image of order, too, cannot survive indefinitely but must shatter on contact with nature, he anticipates that contact and includes it in the artwork itself:

> Stop her there!
> Arms, arms, sword, fire! Corruption in the place!
> False justicer, why hast thou let her 'scape?
>   (54–56)

The defendants escape and the trial breaks down in confusion, as, within its own artificial context, Lear's drama depicts the disruption of its frame of order by a haphazard, uncontrollable intrusion of disorder. In this way, by preempting its confrontation with reality, Lear's artwork not only recognizes its limitations as art but aesthetically masters reality to an unprecedented extent by artificially encompassing it. Despite the frustrated exhaustion into which Lear now subsides once again, he has achieved a kind of success in his agonized struggle to order experience, for his latest vision has not been annihilated by the presence of a contradictory reality. Rather, the play-trial has imaged a moral order violated and overwhelmed, though neither discredited nor negated, by the world's chaotic circumstances; and the fiction of the trial has thus been enabled as an artwork to endure truthfully in the face of the worst that reality can bring to bear.

And so Lear's agonistic effort, in its increasingly artificial mode, has assumed not only the impulse but the generic form of drama, thereby defining and illuminating in a particular way the genesis and possibilities of dramatic art in a chaotic world. We have seen Lear's imaginative works grow in substance and effect proportionally as they were informed with the morality of love and as they included a community in their aesthetic format. At the same time, however, that growth has been accompanied and enabled by an increasing recognition of the limitations of artificial order in dealing with real disorder. Much of the efficacy of the play-trial and the stability of the image of moral order it sets forth derives from its participants' awareness that they are enacting not a real trial but a ritual imitation of a trial, and from the artwork's formal recognition of the chaotic realities over which it has no material power.

These aesthetic considerations are to be sharply confirmed by the implications of Edgar's dramatic artistry. Significantly, Lear begins his long absence from the stage immediately after the play-trial and returns to offset Edgar's dramatic image of order with the chaotic truths of his own experience. Edgar's art is invalidated because it has not recognized its limitations. It attempts to supplant reality entirely with its own illusion, neither defining itself overtly as an artwork nor taking cognizance of any experiential data outside its carefully wrought structure of moral order. It is, therefore, quite vulnerable to the disordered realities of existence as Lear relates them.

In his agonized account at Dover of "how this world goes," Lear is solely concerned to express and cry out against the extremity of suffering and injustice to which he and all men are subject. The limited artistic success of his own efforts to bring some sense of order to life on the great stage of fools is of no relevance to him at this point, for he is preoccupied with the outrageous conditions, which art cannot alter, prevailing over that stage. Yet the increasing sophistication and wisdom of Lear's acts of artistry and the body of aesthetic criteria that has emerged out of them remain of considerable importance to the play itself, adumbrating its very form and purpose. And we are ready, now, to employ what we have learned from both Lear's and Edgar's dramatic works as a perspective on Shakespeare's management of the climax and outcome of *King Lear* itself.

IV

Lear has shown us, in IV.vi., the respect in which "Nature's above art" (86): the material primacy of a disordered nature over man's created forms of order—aesthetic and societal. But Cordelia's Gentleman, before he exits in pursuit of Lear, tells us that Lear has one daughter,

> Who redeems nature from the general curse
> Which twain have brought her to.
>
> (207–208)

And, indeed, the following scene seems to translate Lear's and our own sensibilities to a redeemed world, an entirely different one from that in which the play has hitherto taken place. Lear at first regards what he sees as an apparition of Heaven in the depths of Hell. Yet the world of Cordelia's camp is organized by the very moral imperative which Lear has discovered through his darkest experience—her battle cry is "love, dear love" (IV.iv.28)—and thus the sense of order that has emerged progressively throughout the play is fully realized in the reunion of Lear and Cordelia. It was Cordelia, in fact, who first confronted Lear with a true definition of love, and in banishing her he rejected it as well. Since then, he has attained and internalized love's morality on a far greater scale than that of the parent-child bond he originally broke; and now, in the re-establishment of that bond, all his growth through physical suffering and metaphysical struggle is rewarded by an entire, affirmative vision of love's order. His prayer (III.iv.27–36)—not to the great Gods but to his fellow men—is recalled as he and Cordelia kneel in an explicitly religious recognition of one another, each asking and bestowing blessing:

> *Cordelia.*   O!   look upon me, Sir,
> And hold your hand in benediction o'er me.
> No, Sir, you must not kneel.
>
> (IV.vii.57–59)

After this act of reverence toward Cordelia, whom he does not initially know but worships on the basis of her radiant humanity alone, Lear returns to the problem that has occupied him throughout the play—that of identifying and defining himself. His agony began with the question "Who is it that can tell me who I am?" (I.iv.238), and his subsequent contest with the storm's chaos has been largely an attempt to find or create a structure of meaning by which he might answer that question. Now such a structure is available, and tentative answers begin to emerge:

> I am a very foolish, fond old man,
> Fourscore and upward, not an hour more or less
>
> .   .   .   .
>
>   Do not laugh at me;
> For, as I am a man, I think this lady
> To be my child Cordelia.
>
> *Cordelia.*   And so I am, I am.
>
>   (60–61; 68–70)

In reforging the bond between himself and Cordelia, Lear conclusively defines and affirms his own being even as he identifies his loved one. Ruskin has appropriately commented that "all of Cordelia is poured forth in the infinite 'I am' of fulfilled love." [18] But this is true of Lear as well; he has found in love the recognition and ratification of identity which he originally sought in the macrocosmic order of the Gods; both he and Cordelia now have access to an order that makes possible an "I am," for she is once more his child, and he is again her father—not by all the operation of the orbs but as he is a man: by his integral worth as a human being, expressed and confirmed through the order of love.

This climactic realization of the play's moral order is enclosed in a context of overtly artificial order. The entire action is presided over by the Doctor, an artificer who can directly control and improve nature in the sphere of man's physical being.[19] The optimism implicit in such a profession is applied in a broader context as the Doctor becomes a

kind of dramatic artificer as well, physically directing Lear and Cordelia through each part of their encounter and calling for music—an artificial ordering of time and sound that in turn implies the universal
harmony of the spheres—to accompany the moral and emotional harmony of the event. In this way the action gathers to itself an increasingly formal and ritualistic focus, culminating in the entirely static and
symmetrical stage image of Lear and Cordelia kneeling to each other,
a visual emblem highly charged with representative meaning. The play
thus frames and celebrates the peak of its dramatic order. Lear's discovery of love (along with the self-knowledge and compassion that
made that discovery possible) has been wrested from the turmoil of his
experience and wrought into an aesthetically perfect image of moral
order, an image which seems to resolve all the chaos and dissonance
that have gone before it. Human art, acting as a vehicle for human
morality, seems to have overcome the material and metaphysical chaos
of existence and so redeemed the cursed state of nature.

But the play, of course, does not conclude here. On the contrary,
this scene's perfect image of order will be overturned and shattered by
the chaotic rush of events that actually does conclude the play. And
we have grounds now, Shakespeare's own grounds, to understand why
this will happen. For the image presented by the reunion of Lear and
Cordelia is one of selective order; it relies for its unbroken symmetry
not only on the real experience of love that informs it but as well on
the exclusion of other equally and undeniably real elements of experience. Cordelia, in her militant innocence, cannot comprehend, as we
have, the sense of a confrontation with the ultimate ambiguities of existence that has motivated Lear's agon in the storm:

> Was this a face
> To be oppos'd against the warring winds?
> To stand against the deep dread-bolted thunder?
> In the most terrible and nimble stroke
> Of quick, cross lightning? to watch—poor *perdu!*—
> With this thin helm?
> .   .   .   .

> And wast thou fain, poor father,
> To hovel thee with swine and rogues forlorn,
> In short and musty straw? Alack, alack!
>   (31–36, 38–40)

The metaphysical implications of the struggle never occur to her; she can only regard it as a monstrously inappropriate and pathetic spectacle, one which she would have prevented. Moreover, Lear's own serenity at this point is made possible only through his sleep-induced forgetfulness, a merciful anaesthetic that has temporarily blotted the experience of the storm from his mind. The Doctor specifically warns Cordelia that Lear's "great rage" (78) is only provisionally killed, since "it is danger/To make him even o'er the time he has lost" (79–80).

The fact is that the time Lear has lost contains a number of glaring truths that would annihilate his present tranquillity. For though Lear and Cordelia have risen, by their love, above the bestial, competitive logic of Goneril and Regan—Cordelia harboring "no cause, no cause" (75) not to love Lear in spite of the harm he has done her—they are in no way exempted from being victims of that logic or of the amoral, chaotic nature out of which it arises. The peace and security they enjoy is made possible only by their worldly accommodation, their armed might. And the natural universe is no less indifferent to Lear now that he has learned to love than when it first made nothing of his white hairs. He has fresh garments on him now, but were he still a poor, naked wretch his sufferings would still be undiminished and inseparable from those of a bare, forked animal.

Therefore, in terms of the aesthetics which the play itself has set forth, the reunion of Lear and Cordelia cannot validly serve as the ultimate dramatic image of *King Lear*. For we inhabit a disordered world, and the final complex of visual and emotional meaning with which the play leaves us must confront the truths of our own existence in that world. By excluding the darker aspects of experience as we know them and as the play itself has accurately reflected them, the emblem of Lear and Cordelia tranquilly kneeling in mutual reverence has rendered itself powerless to endure in the face of our world, just as Edgar's and all but the last (the play-trial in III.vi.) of Lear's fictive images of order have been powerless to endure the persistent realities of the play's world. In each instance, the configuration of moral order which the image conveys loses its authority beyond the artificial sphere of the image itself.

Accordingly, Shakespeare forgoes the artistic option which his sources afford him of a romantic, harmonious conclusion, and his play proceeds purposefully and systematically to demolish the perfect image of order which its own artifice has crystallized. By an unexplained, purely haphazard stroke of fortune, Cordelia loses her battle. There is no sense here, as in many Shakespearean battles, of an historical event endowed with moral meaning or of character manifested in conflict. We never even learn why she loses it, since it occurs anticlimactically offstage; out of its distant welter of sound and fury emerges only a single, unexplained piece of data: "King Lear hath lost, he and his daughter ta'en" (V.ii.6). It is a haphazard event in a haphazard world. And this, of course, is not the ultimate calamity. Finally Cordelia herself, the being whose existence, we have been told, redeems nature from its curse, is to be annihilated by a further chaotic and uncontrolled series of events. Nature's above art in that respect.

Just as Lear deliberately enacted the breaking-up of his dramatized trial, then, so Shakespeare anticipates the most devastating possible confrontation between the order of his artwork and the chaos of reality by incorporating that confrontation into the body of the artwork itself. In each case, by structuring into his drama a recognition of the elements of existence which his art can neither control nor alter, the artist enables his drama to meet with and remain valid in the face of those elements. Here, of course, our own emotions and expectations are far more directly involved. The art of *King Lear* itself, not that of a character within the play, is being tried by reality; and we must share in the pain of the ordeal, witnessing the vision of moral order which the play has presented to us subjected to the worst that we know in our own experience: not only human malevolence but worse—blind bad luck. The perfect emblem of the radiant Cordelia kneeling face to face with the reclothed and regenerate Lear is to be smashed before our eyes. Yet whatever survives that smashing will survive in our minds the transition from Shakespeare's play into extradramatic reality. Along with the play itself we are earning, by this ordeal, the right to establish some valid connection between Shakespeare's created world and the world we inhabit.

Prior to Lear's final entrance in the play, all the members of the play-world's surviving community become increasingly united in an effort to accomplish a concrete affirmation of universal order that will explain and bring to a harmonious close the tide of events enveloping them. With Albany's help, Edgar arranges and successfully engages in a trial by combat which (though it is unnecessary since Albany has already uncovered Edmund's guilt and stripped him of power) justifies Edgar's faith in divine providence to the extent that he can refer to the blinding of his father as proof that "the Gods are just" (V.iii.170) in thus punishing adultery. The statement is almost obscenely incongruous; we have watched Gloucester lose his eyes, and we know that, while Edmund contributed to and permitted the act, its more direct cause was Gloucester's own moral choice to comfort and save the life of Lear even if at the expense of his own (III.iii.18–20). Yet any assumption of just cause and effect, no matter how far-fetched, which encompasses events with a sense of cosmic meaning and order, is humanly preferable to recognizing the obvious haphazardness of those events. For the same reason, Albany is quick to seize upon the fates of Goneril and Regan as a "judgment of the heavens" (V.iii.231), although their deaths are a finite instance of what he has feared as a result of the heavens' continued non-intervention: the spectacle of humanity preying on itself "like monsters of the deep" (IV.ii.49).

This communal effort to realize an affirmative denouement reaches its culmination as Edmund is moved to endow his own chaotic end with an unconscious parody of positive meaning:

> Yet Edmund was belov'd:
> The one the other poisoned for my sake,
> And after slew herself.
>
> (V.iii.239–241)

With this inspiration he attempts a melodramatic recantation, revealing his death warrant. But it is, of course, too late. All these efforts, recalling as they do the earlier attempt by Edgar to superimpose an artificial illusion of order directly upon the patent facts of chaos, once more indicate by negatives the necessity of the ordeal by reality to which the play's art is subjecting itself. For in spite of the sincerity in which they are undertaken, all these latter attempts are self-deceptive and ultimately destructive. The delay they cause allows just enough time for the hanging of Cordelia, and Albany's prayer, "The Gods defend her!" (255), is met by the entrance of Lear, his daughter in his arms.

Cordelia is dead, and her death is a colossal non sequitur that assumes the combined weight of all the chaos with which Lear has wrestled: the suffering and bestial condition of man, the atavistic logic of nature, and the indifference of a universe that has neither ratified nor tolerated the human order of love forged in its midst. There is to be no resolution, then, of the play's ongoing dialectic with disorder; the action returns, at its end, to an agonistic level, as Lear raises his voice once more in a final, all-encompassing protest, as eloquent as it is primal and monosyllabic:

> Howl, howl, howl!
> (257)

But this last agony is not limited to Lear alone. His howl, as the lines that follow it make clear, is phrased not only as a personal utterance but as an imperative:

> O! you are men of stones:
> Had I your tongues and eyes, I'd use them so
> That heaven's vault should crack.
> (257–259)

Lear demands that the outcry be a general one on the part of the gathered community onstage and, implicitly, in the audience—that we all recognize and protest the death of Cordelia as the epitome not only

of Lear's but of our own suffering conditions. And the onstage community, all its illusions of order painfully shattered, responds to Lear's
entrance with a choric, almost ritual fulfillment of his demand:

> *Kent.*   Is this the promised end?
> *Edgar.*   Or image of that horror?
> *Albany.*   Fall and cease.
>
>   (263–264)

They formally recognize the sight of Lear and Cordelia as a representative image, for the death of Cordelia, encompassing as it does the
chaos of all existence, points toward the promised end and last horror
of that existence: Armageddon, the final holocaust. Death is the only
absolute and universal certainty of life; as surely as we came crying
hither we are bound obscurely hence, and "This great world/," as
Gloucester has said, "Shall so wear out to nought" (IV.vi.136–137).

Yet all this is only part of the proper impact created by Lear's
final action and speeches. He dies protesting and urging protest, and in
that protest is an important, even a victorious, sense of affirmation.
For Lear ultimately refuses the alternatives that frustration and despair
have repeatedly threatened to force upon him: passive silence or,
worse, a nihilistic acceptance of things as they are. He has learned far
too much of a positive nature to negate it all now, and in this, his ultimate confrontation with suffering and disorder, he clings firmly to
the moral order of love which he has achieved in his struggle and fulfilled in his reunion with Cordelia. His sense of the human worth and
identity which love affords is undiminished in his last magnificent
surge:

> And my poor fool is hanged! No, no, no life!
> Why should a dog, a horse, a rat have life,
> And thou no breath at all?
>
>   (V.iii.305–307)

For the final time, he fiercely insists that man's life is not cheap as
beast's, even as he challenges the inherent terms of existence which,

as shown by Cordelia's death, make no distinction between the two. Lear is still determined to crack heaven's vault for this dichotomy. Like Albert Camus' "metaphysical rebel," he affirms to the end "an assessment of values" in the name of which he "refuses to accept the condition in which he finds himself." [20] And in demanding that the theatrical community share in his protest he has invited them to share in his affirmation as well. In the face of the worst possible denouement, the play's moral order has endured.

There is, besides, an important visual dimension to this last sequence, one which circumscribes the action's verbal meaning and resolves the aesthetic issues that have concerned us throughout this essay. Lear's entering imperative to the community demands not only a vocal but a visual response: the use of "eyes" as well as "tongues" (258); and his last words in the play emphatically repeat that demand:

> Do you see this? Look at her, look, her lips,
> Look there, look there!
>
> (310–311)

I am unconvinced by Bradley's interpretation of these lines as expressing Lear's delusion that Cordelia is alive; this seems to me profoundly out of context. [21] Rather, I would suggest that the primary significance here lies in Lear's emphasis on visual cognition. The sight which, with his last breath, Lear calls on us to "see" and "look upon" has been the focal point of a central, static, stage picture for some time now, the object of all eyes onstage as well as in the audience. Edgar has overtly pronounced the dead Cordelia in the arms of the dying Lear an "image" (264), and Albany has broken off his own discourse with "O! see, see!" (304). Edgar and Albany, along with the rest of the play's characters, have arranged themselves in a kind of onstage audience, their attention fixed, like ours, entirely on Lear and Cordelia. After all this, Lear's insistence on our "seeing" must evoke from us a self-consciousness of our own roles as spectators, an awareness that we have an aesthetic as well as an emotional relationship to the image before us.

Thus Shakespeare isolates and frames the unmoving, *pietà* tableau of Lear and Cordelia, presenting it for our communal recognition as the play's ultimate dramatic image. That image, in its total desolation, reflects the worst realities of our own experience, realities which art cannot prevent or change. Yet it also reflects undiminished the order that the play's art has devised to confront those realities. Its visual composition shows Lear and Cordelia together, no less together than in the similarly static and framed image of their reunion which this supplants. Cordelia is in Lear's arms, more his child now than ever, and Lear is massive with the dignity of his fatherhood. Shakespeare has thus come to terms with the aesthetic problem which he has posed and explored throughout the play. The order of love has survived the transition, imposed by the play's art upon itself, from the context of pure artifice surrounding the image of Lear and Cordelia reunited to the context of absolute reality surrounding the image of Lear and Cordelia dead. It is the latter, a dark and painful emblem, which *King Lear* finally holds up to us; but by its unrelenting reflection of the real world's chaos that image retains the integrity necessary to communicate into our world an uncompromised vision of moral order.

Chapter Three

THE ART ITSELF IS NATURE: "THE WINTER'S TALE"

I

Although *King Lear* and *The Winter's Tale* are separated chronologically by at least four other plays, a number of shared and complementary elements suggest that the two works be considered in tandem. As paradigmatic realizations of their two contrasting yet related genres, they might even be termed companion pieces. Instinctively, one thinks of *King Lear* as the fullest realization of Shakespeare's tragic impulse, and certainly *The Winter's Tale*—though *The Tempest* is ultimately, perhaps, a play of more profound vision—represents Shakespeare's richest and most comprehensive use of the tragicomic romance form. Reaping the full benefit of the experimental cartoons, *Pericles* and *Cymbeline,* that precede it, *The Winter's Tale* fully works out its form's pattern of movement from error, chaos, and separation toward repentence, regeneration, and reunion, elevating it to the level of an integral and far-reaching work of art. E. M. W. Tillyard's remarks are especially appropriate:

It is almost as if he aimed at rendering the complete theme of *The Divine Comedy.* Indeed, it is not fantastic to see in *The Winter's Tale* Shakespeare's attempt to compress that whole theme into a single play through the direct presentation of all its parts. . . .

Being all-inclusive and doing justice to what it includes, *The Winter's Tale* stands by itself, a microcosm.[1]

It is not surprising, then, in view of the work's nature as a definitive essay in Shakespeare's final dramatic genre, that we find in the fabric of *The Winter's Tale* the element which has been the focus of our study of *King Lear:* Shakespeare's concern to define the aesthetic and moral relevance of his art to reality, to establish through the artwork itself a vital relationship between the created world onstage and the surrounding world of the audience. As in *King Lear,* he accomplishes this end primarily through representative attempts by characters within the play to cope with or alter the circumstances of reality in their own world directly through exercises of dramatic artifice. But *The Winter's Tale,* while addressing itself to many of the same problems we have examined in *King Lear,* devotes itself to shaping an antithetically positive and confident solution to them.

For instance, in the final two acts of *The Winter's Tale* we find a series of incidents comparable to Edgar's dramatic artistry at Dover. In IV.iv., Camillo conceives of a plan for Florizel's and Perdita's escape to Sicilia. They are to present themselves before Leontes, performing actions and reciting dialogue entirely composed by Camillo:

> The manner of your bearing towards him, with
> What you (as from your father) shall deliver,
> Things known betwixt us three, I'll write you down:
> The which shall point you forth at every setting
> What you must say; that he shall not perceive
> But that you have your father's bosom there
> And speak his very heart.[2]
>
> (559–565)

The scenario that Camillo thus writes down calls for the young couple to play roles in an image of reality that is a desirable but illusory vision of his imagining: they are to announce that Florizel has married with his father's consent, that Perdita is a king's daughter, and that all is well once again between Sicilia and Bohemia. As the actions and

language of the characters further make clear, the event planned is to
be nothing less than a work of drama. Camillo even acquires costumes
and promises more properties for the project's final act:

> it shall be so my care
> To have you royally appointed as if
> The scene you play were mine.
>   (592–594)

And Perdita observes,

> I see the play so lies
> That I must bear a part.
>   (655–656)

Like Edgar's delusion of Gloucester, though, this is drama not in the
overt context of a play but of an attempt to shape reality directly
through art; Leontes is to be convinced that the fiction played out
before him is factual. In the following scene, as the lovers gain an audience and execute their parts, Leontes, like Gloucester, fully and
gladly accepts as truth the illusion he witnesses. But then, just as the
mad Lear rushed in to shatter the optimism of Edgar's morality-play
image of the world, a Lord runs breathlessly into Leontes' court to expose and dispel the artifice of Florizel and Perdita, announcing that
Florizel is a truant of whom his father is in outraged pursuit and that
Perdita, a "seeming lady" (V.i.190), is in reality not a princess but a
shepherd's daughter.

   In each incident, then, a character's attempt to create and foster
by dramatic art a desirable, ordered illusion of reality is broken in
upon and apparently discredited by the evidence of reality itself. But
here the parallel ceases. Leontes, confronting the gap between the artificial and the actual, nevertheless decides, after an unrehearsed plea
by Florizel, to undertake the cause of the lovers as their protector and
advocate—to help the illusion he has witnessed become, in a partial
sense at least, a reality. Immediately following this decision, as we

learn in the next scene, a seemingly miraculous chain of meetings, revelations, and recognitions occurs, the net result of which is that every element in Camillo's dramatic vision does in fact become literal reality: Perdita *is* the daughter of a king, Leontes' daughter, the betrothal of the lovers is blessed by all, and the two kings Sicilia and Bohemia are joyfully reunited. Moreover, Leontes' heir restored, the way is paved for the culminating reunion of Leontes and Hermione. Thus Camillo's exercise of dramatic art has indeed influenced the condition of the real world, apparently reforming that world to fit its own artificial image. The gap between the ideal order of art and the chaos of reality, which invalidated Edgar's dramatic endeavors and with which the art of *King Lear* itself came to terms only through a formal recognition of its own inability to alter reality, has here been bridged and crossed. Not only has Camillo's artificial image been successfully substituted for reality, but it has literally *become* reality.

We shall return to consider Camillo's project in depth and detail, but even this cursory treatment suggests some preliminary observations. Just as the invalidation of Edgar's artistry served as a *via negativa* for the art of the play *King Lear,* so the success of Camillo's drama affords us a significant perspective not only on the role of dramatic art within the play's world but on the art of *The Winter's Tale* itself. For the "real" world which Camillo's drama reforms from within is itself Shakespeare's own dramatic image of a world, and we, the inhabitants of the real world outside Shakespeare's play, are audience to that image just as Leontes has been audience to Camillo's. The crucial significance of Leontes' willingness to convert the dramatic image he has witnessed to a reality thus implies the possibility of a parallel relationship between ourselves and Shakespeare's artwork.

Looking to the play's one formal speech of extradramatic address, Time's Chorus at the start of Act IV, we find that parallel reenforced. By this point it will have become quite clear to us that the play is deeply rooted in the generic area of romance, where, as opposed to the world of *Lear,* "certain moral and magical laws are held constant and fully effective for the purpose of subordinating accident and evil." [3] Yet Time admits of no such convention. Gower, in his choric speeches and dumbshows, studiously maintained the boundary between the elaborate romantic artifice of *Pericles* and the world of its audience, repeatedly calling the spectators back to their own norm of reality as from a pleasant fantasy, a venerable old tale whose moral messages could be neatly separated from their fictional and illusory contexts. But Time, while explaining to the audience a lapse of sixteen years in the plot, makes no distinction between dramatic time and real time; neither does he, like Gower and most other Shakespearean choruses, make reference to the objective untruth of the onstage action. Rather, "in the name of Time" (IV.Cho.3), he takes it upon himself to present the events of *The Winter's Tale* as a true work of time, a temporal reality. Simultaneously he does not avoid presenting the play overtly as a work of dramatic art, a theatrical event. He addresses us specifically as an audience, "gentle spectators" (20), with all the deference that marks other such speeches in Shakespeare's works; he describes himself as turning his glass in order to "give my scene . . . growing" (16); and he refers to an earlier piece of exposition in the play—"I mentioned a son o' th' king's" (22)—as his own utterance. Thus, far from distinguishing between the artifice of the play and the reality of the audience's world, Time offers us a perspective on the play both as an artwork and as a reality: the creation either of a playwright who takes upon himself the name of Time, or of a cosmic condition, Time itself, which operates according to a plan of dramatic artifice. We are, then, being encouraged to respond to Shakespeare's play interchangeably as artifice and as reality, to "impute it not a crime" (4) if our normal expectations in this area are surprised or overturned.

On both levels of *The Winter's Tale,* then, within and without the play, we encounter a new and confident relationship between art and reality, and in order to understand that relationship as it emerges through the body of the play, we will examine the nature of the play's world; the full genesis, success, and significance of Camillo's artistry within that world; and finally the culminating work of art by a character in the play: Paulina's unveiling and transformation of Hermione's statue, which in a single theatrical event aligns the function of dramatic art within the play's world with the dramatic art of the play itself, effecting a vital and conclusive definition of both. And we will find, in that definition, the lineaments of an absolute and inclusive artistic statement that is superseded only by that of *The Tempest*.

II

The proportions and values of the world imaged by *The Winter's Tale* are defined at its outset by Camillo in his conversation with Archidamus:

Sicilia cannot show himself overkind to Bohemia. They were trained together in their childhoods, and there rooted between them then such an affection which cannot choose but branch now. Since their more mature dignities and royal necessities made separation of their society, their encounters, though not personal, have been royally attorneyed with interchange of gifts, letters, loving embassies, that they have seemed to be together, though absent; shook hands, as over a vast; and embraced, as it were, from the ends of opposed winds. The heavens continue their loves!

(I.i.21–32)

Unlike the bleak Britain of Lear, from which the dominion of the loving France was remote and invisible, this is a world containing two countries and two kings, a world whose whole structure rests almost physically on a universal bond of love: that between Leontes and Polixenes, which in turn figures the love among the peoples of Sicilia and Bohemia. Camillo's imagery implies that love is the organizing principle, not only of the play's human sector, but of all its natural universe as well. Love stretches "over a vast" and "from the ends of opposed winds"; affection has "rooted" and "cannot choose but branch now." By the same imperative that a tree must grow, Sicilia and Bohemia must love.

The world that subsequently passes before our eyes entirely realizes this image: a world in which human and non-human nature are fully reconciled in one moral order, the "law and process of great nature" (II.ii.60), based on love in all its forms, particularly as they apply to the continuum of regenerative processes by which all of nature renews itself. The opening scenes are redolent with love and generation: the elaborately graceful rituals of courtesy and compliment among the princes and lords of Sicilia and Bohemia, the narration of Leontes' courtship of Hermione, the youthful presence of Mamillius, and the sense of hopeful expectancy centered on Hermione's pregnancy. All that lives in this world moves harmoniously to natural rhythms of love; love of the old for the young is a bodily and spiritual panacea that "physics the subject, makes old hearts fresh" (I.i.38–39), and "cures . . . / Thoughts that would thick [Polixenes'] blood" (I.ii.170–171). As to sexual love, the very gods, as Florizel will tell Perdita, are as motivated as men and animals by attraction for kind and the urge to perpetuate life, "humbling their deities to love":

> Jupiter
> Became a bull, and bellow'd; the green Neptune
> A ram, and bleated; and the fire-rob'd god,
> Golden Apollo, a poor humble swain.
>   (IV.iv.25–30)

Thus nature is infused with divinity and divinity is inseparable from nature. Apollo, the very god who austerely passes judgment on Leontes' acts of hate, is bound no less than his subject by the natural imperative of love.

In short, the world-image of *The Winter's Tale* focuses on the same experiential elements as that of *King Lear* but from an opposing perspective. Lear's discovery that a sense of order could be affirmed in human love in spite of man's natural condition has been converted to a universal vision of natural and moral order. Like Lear in his banishment of Cordelia, Leontes will initiate a period of chaos by denying the bonds of love between himself and his fellows, casting out his child as a bastard, divorcing his wife as an adulteress, and attempting to murder his friend. But while Lear had to confront not only his own misdeeds but the greater chaos, moral and elemental, of the world he inhabited, Leontes will meet with the unambiguous retribution of the cosmic order he has outraged. Not only will the responsible spokesmen of human society oppose and condemn his course of action, but the natural universe itself will react to punish his violation of its laws and to heal the gash he has made in its fabric. Lear encountered in the storm a blind chaos of wind and rain that afflicted all the naked, unaccommodated creatures exposed to it. Conversely, Leontes will expose Perdita to a storm which will, he expects, blindly destroy her; instead, it will prove the instrument of an immanently moral nature, ruthlessly destroying all who have executed Leontes' chaotic will and carefully preserving Perdita to grow and prosper in Bohemia.

Man's fictive arts, as attempts to give form and order to a disordered reality, are initially absent from the world of *The Winter's Tale;* the creation of artificial images of order by illusion is unnecessary when a vital frame of moral order is everywhere evident in human and non-human nature. Thus, when Leontes first threatens that order, his chief moral counsellors Camillo and Paulina, who will later become the play's principal artist figures, simply iterate to him without artifice or illusion the facts of his world as they are apparent to all but his own crazed consciousness: that Hermione is his faithful wife, Perdita his true daughter, and Polixenes his blameless friend. Camillo unhesitatingly pronounces Leontes' accusation of Hermione a "sin" (I.ii.283), and Paulina charges him with his moral obligations to his child in terms that at once affirm the natural order of love and generation and reflect upon the definition of art within that order. Unveiling Perdita, whom she has presumably concealed in the folds of her mantle, she lays the child before Leontes:

> The good queen
> (For she is good) hath brought you forth a daughter;
> Here 'tis. . . .
>
>   .   .   .   .
>
>   Behold, my lords,
> Although the print be little, the whole matter
> And copy of the father: eye, nose, lip;
> The trick of's frown; his forehead; nay, the valley,

The pretty dimples of his chin and cheek; his smiles;
The very mould and frame of hand, nail, finger;
And thou, good goddess Nature, which hast made it
So like to him that got it, if thou hast
The ordering of the mind too, 'mongst all colours
No yellow in't, lest she suspect, as he does,
Her children not her husband's!
                                                    (II.iii.64–66, 97–107)

Paulina's first significant action in the play, like her last, is thus her unveiling to Leontes—in the context of a work of fictive art—a human being whom he is obliged to recognize and love. Just as she will present Hermione in the guise of a statue, she here refers to Perdita as a painting, a "print" of Leontes. But while she will present Hermione as a product of human art, the statue of Julio Romano, here she credits the "good goddess Nature" herself as the artist. For there is no gap, in this as yet unfallen world, between the perfect order of art and the continuum of reality sculpted by nature. As long as all moves in harmony with nature, nature, by its dynamic order of love and generation, shapes an entirely ordered existence. No other fictive artist is necessary: nature itself is the artist.

But the human world of *The Winter's Tale* does fall into chaos by falling out of concord with nature, and it is in the face of this chaos that the human artistry of Camillo and Paulina will evolve. Leontes' imprisonment of Hermione and banishment of Perdita are the immediate causes of this disorder, but both these actions derive from a single fault in Leontes deeper than either sexual jealousy or paternal irresponsibility: that is, a total lapse of faith. Surrounded by the patent and unfeigned evidence of order and goodness in his world, Leontes simply ceases to believe that world to be either ordered or good. His course is, in this sense, again an exact inversion of Lear's. Lear began his tragic career with naive confidence in his own, divinely enforced security within an ordered universe, arriving only after an agonizing confrontation with universal disorder and corruption at his scathing denunciation of existence, rife with sexual nausea, in the fourth act.

Leontes, however, begins with all of Lear's disgust and disillusionment, though nothing in his world beyond his own twisted psyche justifies or confirms his attitude. The very textures of his diction and rhythms of his speech clash grotesquely with the serenity of the dialogue surrounding his:

> Physic for't there's none:
> It is a bawdy planet, that will strike
> Where 'tis predominant; and 'tis powerful, think it,
> From east, west, north, south; be it concluded,
> No barricado for a belly. Know't,
> It will let in and out the enemy,
> With bag and baggage: many thousand on's
> Have the disease, and feel't not.
>
> (I.ii.200–207)

While the chaotic elements of his universe made nothing of Lear and his little world of man, Leontes, revelling in nothing, actively seeks out of his private chaos to deny and annihilate the vitally ordered cosmos around him:

> is this nothing?
> Why then the world, and all that's in't, is nothing,
> The covering sky is nothing, Bohemia nothing,
> My wife is nothing, nor nothing have these nothings,
> If this be nothing.
>
> (I.ii.292–296)

And to a considerable extent, he succeeds, if not in proving his world corrupt, yet in destroying much of its goodness and seriously warping its frame of order. He breaks the bond with Bohemia, loses his wife and daughter, and forces himself and Sicilia to "live without an heir," on the brink of nothing in other words, "if that which is lost be not found" (III.ii.135–136).

The world of *The Winter's Tale* thus becomes an imperfect, fallen one as a direct result of Leontes' refusal to believe it otherwise, his determination to believe in nothing: "All's true that is mistrusted" (II.i.48) is his cry as he first unveils his obsession to the court at large. Polixenes, too, presages his later repetition of Leontes' sin (in opposing the love of Florizel and Perdita and in threatening to cast out his son) by betraying a similar mistrust in the inherent goodness and moral integrity of nature's procreative cycles when he avers that he and Leontes lost the pastoral purity of their childhoods in encountering the "temptations" (I.ii.77) of their wives. Hermione's immediate reproof is more than a playful one, for in terming lawful sexual union a lapse from goodness Polixenes has, by implication, denied the goodness of great nature's law and process no less than will Leontes in condemning Hermione's chaste vitality as wanton lust and his own child as a bastard.

Lack of faith, then—unbelief in the inherent goodness and order of things—is the central destructive force in this play's world; and the essence of that faithlessness is realized in Leontes' response to Paulina's unveiling of Perdita. Paulina has formally—almost theatrically—confronted him with nature's work of art, but Leontes refuses to respond to this artifact believingly. Immediately upon her presentation of the child he condemns Paulina as "a mankind witch" (II.iii.67) and threatens death by fire (113), the punishment due to necromancy. Thus he rejects Perdita and the generative, loving order which—work of art and natural fact in one—she embodies, as the product of witchcraft, a perverse, dissembling art of illusions. With this aesthetic rejection, he irrevocably alienates the little world of man from the law and process of great nature, initiating a time of chaos in which the data of that world will no longer conform to the encompassing order of nature's art. Ironically, it will indeed be an art of illusions—the art of drama—that will play a key role in restoring Leontes' world to its original harmony with the order of nature. And of that art, not far removed from witchcraft in its ability to conjure up living images, Leontes will be brought to say, "If this be magic, let it be an art/Lawful as eating" (V.iii.110–111).

III

While the human world of *The Winter's Tale* falls into disorder, nature remains, in itself, ordered and unfallen. As we have already seen, natural forces intervene on the seacoast of Bohemia to preserve Perdita, the seed, the "blossom" (III.iii.46) that is indispensable to nature's regenerative cycle. That seed is planted and—fostered by two naturals, the Shepherd and the Clown—attains a blooming maturity in the verdant landscape of Bohemia. It is also by natural forces—the flight of a falcon (IV.iv.15-16) and the inclinations of youthful blood—that the opportunity arises for the seed to bear fruit in the union of Perdita and Florizel, the potential salvation of the play's fallen human world. But nature alone can do no more than create such a potential. Leontes has rejected nature's artistry in Sicilia, and Polixenes will soon repeat that rejection in Bohemia. Nature can accomplish its own generative cycles, but man's social order no longer moves in harmony with those cycles; and nature unaided cannot convey its fruitful seed of order back into human society. As a human lapse of faith has alienated the world of man from the frame of nature, so it must be by human art that the societies of Bohemia and Sicilia are once again aligned with great nature's law and process. The definition of such an art emerges and evolves, simultaneously with the unfolding of Perdita's and Florizel's love, in the "great middle" of the play (to borrow V. A. Kolve's term for its structural counterpart, the storm sequence, in *King Lear*),[4] the sheep-shearing scene (iv) of the Fourth Act.

The pastoral mode of the scene prepares us by convention for a perspective on the relationship of human art to nature, and at its center is the debate of Polixenes and Perdita over the moral question of humanly-grafted flowers. The aesthetic implications of this passage and of the scene as a whole have been much discussed as Shakespeare's contribution to the Renaissance art-versus-nature issue,[5] and while this aspect of the scene is as important as it is self-evident, I do not propose to treat it here in any depth. For the aesthetics of the scene

serve an even more important function by introducing the artistic principles that will determine the role of drama in the play: not only dramatic art as it is practiced in the world of the play but the art of *The
Winter's Tale* itself.

Perdita begins her argument with Polixenes by refusing to plant
"nature's bastards" (83), carnations and streaked gillyvors, because
"There is an art which, in their piedness, shares/With great creating
nature" (87–88). A true foster-child of nature, she is innocent of the
human fall from order that followed her birth. Her perspective on
human artistry is the same as that which Paulina inferred in the yet-un-
fallen time when she presented to Leontes nature's work of art, Perdita
herself: that since nature is the controlling artist of man's existence, it
is neither necessary nor proper for man to rival nature by attempting,
through his own arts, to shape or alter the stuff of that existence. But
Polixenes offers a maturer point of view. He justifies the application of
human art directly to nature on the grounds that

> nature is made better by no mean
> But nature makes that mean: so, over that art,
> Which you say adds to nature, is an art
> That nature makes. You see, sweet maid, we marry
> A gentler scion to a bark of baser kind
> By bud of nobler race. This is an art
> Which does mend nature—change it rather—but
> The art itself is nature.
>
> (89–97)

A creature of nature reformed and shaped by art is no less natural,
since, nature having originally created the artist, "the art itself is nature." Human artifice, then, is a medium through which nature can
mend, change, and improve itself. The end result is an indirect work
of nature's own art and is therefore not less real because it has been effected by man's artifice.

These principles are contextually realized in terms that apply to
drama increasingly throughout the scene, climaxing in the inception
of Camillo's project. Ironically, both Perdita and Polixenes voice, on

an abstract level, arguments that are contradicted by their principal actions. The scene opens in masquerade and contains, in the informal context of a Whitsuntide celebration, several acts of play and artifice centering on Perdita. She is wearing a queen's costume decorated largely, one presumes, with flowers (since Florizel compares her to Flora, goddess of flowers), and she proceeds to strew all those around her with garlands of flowers proper to the "time of day" (114), the life-stage and qualities, of each: winter flowers for the old, flowers of middle summer for the middle-aged, and flowers of the spring (if she had them) for the young. Anne Righter has observed that these actions move specifically in the direction of drama:

> The year itself seems to die and be born again. Set off from the episodes around it by its formalism and lyrical perfection, the scene represents a kind of play within the play . . .[6]

Here, in any case, we have a dynamic visual metaphor that puts Polixenes' aesthetic directly into practice. Perdita costumes the shepherds and shepherdesses by an artificial arrangement of natural objects, and in so doing she aligns her immediate society with the cycles of nature, embellishing and heightening the natural truths of each rustic's particular existence. And we perceive a deeper significance in her own costume and her player-queen role, for we know that she is in fact a princess, or was one before Leontes' unnatural lapse of faith. Thus by her semidramatic artistry Perdita actualizes nature's deepest truths far more than the artist herself is aware. She feels only a vague uneasiness:

> Methinks I play as I have seen them do
> In Whitsun pastorals: sure this robe of mine
> Does change my disposition.
> (133–135)

Mends it rather: restores it to what it was before the order of art and the data of reality were in any way separate. Working through a natural medium and in accordance with nature's order, Perdita has, like a flower grafter, produced an artwork that attains the validity of a fact in nature. Her art, in changing and mending nature, is itself nature.

But Polixenes shatters the sheep-shearing idyll just as Leontes broke the harmony of the Sicilian court. His offenses are parallel: he attacks the bond of love between Florizel and Perdita, threatens to disown his child, and condemns Perdita as a "piece/Of excellent witchcraft" (424), an "enchantment" (435). Thus Polixenes' ultimate unbelief in the goodness of nature's order is contained, like Leontes', in a rejection of nature's artifact, Perdita, as the product of witchcraft, of a false, illusory art. This repetition of Leontes' sin is the immediate occasion of Camillo's dramatic artwork, which alone precipitates the regenerative tide of events resulting in the restoration of the playworld to its original harmony.

Camillo has been a witness to the debate of Perdita and Polixenes as well as to Perdita's acts of floral art and festive masquerade. However, all the scene's levels of art—the art of nature in Perdita's being and Perdita's human art in the alignment of her pastoral society and herself with nature's order—have been violated and broken off by Polixenes; Perdita herself resolves to abandon her own artifice as an empty "dream," from which, "being now awake, I'll queen it no inch further" (449–450). But Camillo will not allow her to drop her role. Instead, he conceives of a far more elaborate and specifically dramatic project based on the same aesthetic principles. He perceives the natural validity of the bond between Florizel and Perdita in Florizel's defiant resolution to maintain that bond, his entire dedication to nature's order, and his rejection of all in man's fallen order—even, if necessary, reason itself (483–486)—that threatens the fulfillment of his love, which

> cannot fail, but by
> The violation of my faith; and then
> Let nature crush the sides o' th' earth together,
> And mar the seeds within!
>   (477–480)

This unmistakably echoes Lear's invocation that the storm

> Strike flat the thick rotundity o' th' world,
> Crack nature's moulds, all germens spill at once.
> (*King Lear*, III.iii.7–8)

However, like much else in *The Winter's Tale*, Florizel's speech presents an inversion of the corresponding situation in *King Lear*. Lear called down annihilation upon a nature that he found contrary to his own desires, while Florizel identifies his faith and love entirely with the natural order. His love cannot fail until nature destroys its own seeds. Indeed, to capitulate to his father's will would be to allow an attempted marring of nature's generative order, and this Florizel refuses to do.

Thus Camillo, the original spokesman in the play for the cosmic harmony that united the human worlds of Sicilia and Bohemia within nature's vast-spanning order of love, cannot but recognize in Florizel and Perdita the affirmation of all the natural values and regenerative possibilities which Leontes and Polixenes have cast away. Here is a seed too precious to be lost or planted randomly. But Perdita, he assumes, is not a king's daughter, and, the world being what it is, the two cannot maintain their bond of love either openly in Bohemia or haphazardly anywhere else. Accordingly, he plans the artwork whose overtly dramatic, indeed theatrical, proportions we discussed at the outset of this chapter, an artwork involving a direct application in drama of the floral aesthetics suggested by Polixenes and practiced by Perdita. He will arrange Florizel (whose name speaks for itself) and the "blossom" Perdita in an artificial context that images a natural truth: their virtuous and regenerative union—which the conditions of a fallen world have prevented from coming to pass—as it might have been before the world fell from the frame of nature's order. And just as the grafter intends his artificial manipulation of two flowers to take root and grow into a natural fact, Camillo engineers his dramatic image so that it may graduate from illusion to reality. By playing the

roles of husband and wife, the lovers are to attain the security necessary to their actual marriage.

But Camillo's artistic intentions are of a far broader scope than
the accomplishment of a single marriage. His vision of exactly how
Leontes is to respond to this drama makes clear that he sees a definite
possibility not only of Florizel and Perdita fulfilling their bond of love
under Leontes' protection but of Leontes himself redeeming his original violation of nature's order:

> Methinks I see
> Leontes himself opening his free arms and weeping
> His welcomes forth; asks thee there 'Son, forgiveness!'
> As 'twere i' th' father's person; kisses the hands
> Of your fresh princess; o'er and o'er divides him
> 'Twixt his unkindness and his kindness; th' one
> He chides to hell, and bids the other grow
> Faster than thought or time.
>
> (548–555)

By embracing the lovers and, implicitly, recognizing the natural values they embody, Leontes can vicariously undo his own original rejection of those values. And all along we are aware, as Camillo himself is
not, of a deeper natural truth—Perdita's identity as a princess—that
this masquerade will actualize. Since nature's art, which is reality, has
twice been crucially denied as illusion, man's fictive, illusionary art
must now work the means of eradicating that denial.

IV

All these ends, then, are to be accomplished through the medium of a
dramatic presentation before Leontes, and their accomplishment, as
indeed the outcome of *The Winter's Tale* itself, rests not only on the
effectiveness of Camillo's drama but equally on Leontes' response to
it as audience. The next scene's opening dialogue between Leontes

and Paulina establishes that, Cleomenes' opening assertion to the contrary, Leontes has not yet "done enough" (V.i.1), in spite of all his penitence, to undo his original rejection of nature's moral order in Hermione. Thus Camillo's device is further anticipated as a chance for Leontes to re-confront and recognize that order. Significantly, the appearance before him of Florizel and Perdita specifically recapitulates the occasion of Leontes' rejection of the harmony between man's world and nature's law and process, Paulina's presentation to him of Perdita as nature's work of art. In his gracious greeting of the lovers, he applies to Florizel exactly the terms of imitative art that Paulina applied to Perdita:

> Your mother was most true to wedlock, prince;
> For she did print your royal father off
> Conceiving you. Were I but twenty-one,
> Your father's image is so hit in you,
> His very air, that I should call you brother,
> As I did him, and speak of something wildly
> By us perform'd before. Most dearly welcome!
>
> (123–129)

Thus, even before Florizel has launched into his prepared speech, Leontes has affirmed the inherent order and moral validity—the art—of nature's generative process, which he originally condemned as witchcraft. In addition, though none but we, the audience, are aware of it, he has embraced in Perdita the very natural artwork he once cast away. He then goes on to accept joyfully the artificial account (set down by Camillo) which Florizel unfolds to him of the renewed love of Polixenes, the measuring once again of the "lands and waters" between their thrones (143-144), and thus the restoration of the cosmic bond that originally linked Bohemia and Sicilia in natural harmony. Finally, he reveals his own increasing realignment with nature's cyclic order by proclaiming the lovers (and, implicitly, all the harmony and regenerative possibility which Camillo's dramatic image has set forth) as welcome to his court "As is the spring to th' earth" (151). It was through lack of faith in the manifest goodness and natural order of his world that Leontes damaged and disordered that world. Now the product of Camillo's artifice, an image of the world as restored to its original order, has reactivated such a faith, and the restoration of faith makes possible the restoration of order.

It is at this point, however, that Camillo's drama comes to an abrupt end, its illusion shattered by the intrusion of reality in the announcements of the Lord. Leontes is forced by the news of Polixenes' arrival to confront the gap between the dramatic illusion he has so enthusiastically accepted as truth and the harsh facts of the actual world. The ordered world-image set forth by the lovers, a natural harmony of loving relationships, is dispelled by a cacophony of opposition, antipathy, and frustration:

> Bohemia greets you from himself, by me;
> Desires you to attach his son, who has—
> His dignity and duty both cast off—
> Fled from his father, from his hopes, and with
> A shepherd's daughter.
>   .   .   .   .
> [the Clown and Shepherd] kneel, they kiss the earth;
> Forswear themselves as often as they speak.
> Bohemia stops his ears, and threatens them
> With divers deaths in death.
>   (180–184, 198–201)

But this shock, too, has been part of Camillo's original plan: he has engineered the arrival of Polixenes just as he has composed Florizel's speeches. For though Leontes' faith has been awakened, not until he has fully perceived Camillo's drama for what it is, an overtly artificial image of reality, can he act on that faith most meaningfully to eradicate his original acts of chaos. Passive belief in an illusion, such as Edgar attempted to instil in Gloucester, is not sufficient; before he has "done enough" Leontes must, as audience, accept the responsibility of conveying the order of Camillo's created world directly into the disordered world of reality. As Leontes observes with regret that he has witnessed an illusion unlikely, given the conditions of reality, ever to become truth (209–214), Florizel, now an actor out of his part, delivers an impromptu epilogue:

> Beseech you, sir,
> Remember since you ow'd no more to time
> Than I do now: with thought of such affections,
> Step forth mine advocate.
>
> (217–220)

He pleads that Leontes actively contribute to making the events he has witnessed in art come to pass: that he take it on himself to validate the dramatic image he has observed not merely by approving the truth of the moral order it has depicted, but by recognizing and affirming those sectors of his own experience corresponding to that order, making its dynamic impetus his own, and thus acting to restore it in some measure to the world outside Camillo's drama.

Leontes responds fully to this plea, calling up in a very real way the memory of his love for Hermione by showing a more than hospitable interest in Perdita (222). His reply to Paulina's objection that in this he shows "too much youth" (224) is a valid one: "I thought of her [Hermione] / Even as these looks I made" (227). For the first time in the play he affirms the place of nature's generative force within himself, achieving in the memory of his "affections" for Hermione a real rejuvenation. Intent on averting a repetition by Polixenes of the chaos Leontes himself caused, he goes forth, the advocate in the real world of the moral order he has encountered in Camillo's art, to promote the vital union of Florizel and Perdita and to re-establish the bond of love between himself and Polixenes.

Thus the incipient regeneration of Leontes and of his world are synonymous with his decision to eliminate a barrier between art and reality by actualizing a vision of order that has appeared to be overtly fictional. And as an immediate result of this decision, every major detail of that fiction comes wonderfully true far beyond the expectations of its originator, its actors, or its audience. For Camillo's drama becomes literal fact. His artificial grafting of a flower with a blossom takes root and flourishes, as Florizel and Perdita are betrothed with the blessings of all. Leontes and Polixenes embrace again "as over a vast" of sixteen years. The player-princess of the drama proves indeed the daughter of a king, for that which is lost has been found. Love and generation have once more rooted and branched in the societies of Sicilia and Bohemia, as man's order increasingly regains its harmony with nature's. Camillo and Leontes look "as they had heard of a world ransomed, or one destroyed" (V.ii.14–15), for indeed, the original world of the play, eclipsed as it was by Leontes' unbelief, has been ransomed by Camillo's drama and Leontes' response to it.

V

Thus, within the context of its own artificial world, *The Winter's Tale* has defined a vital and organic relationship between a work of dramatic art and the world surrounding it: through unbelief man has fallen from his cosmic harmony with nature's order and the shaping influence of nature's art, but a work of human art imaging the essence of that forsaken order has reawakened man's original belief, providing a medium for the return of nature's order to man's world. And as the reality of man's world conforms once again to nature's law and process, the dramatic artwork evolves to a natural reality. However, the play has yet to achieve a full definition of its own relationship as a work of drama to our world, to the norm of reality defining our own existences outside the boundaries of Shakespeare's created world. Such a definition becomes an increasingly central theme of the play's final two scenes, which establish and ultimately put to trial an implied parallel between dramatic art as it is practiced within the world of the play and the dramatic art of the play itself.

We ourselves do not view the miraculous denouement of Camillo's artistry. Instead we are informed of it at second hand by the relation of the three Gentlemen in V.ii., not only because a scene of so many recognitions and reunions would overload the stage with emotion but because Shakespeare means us to witness the event through the eyes of others: an audience, like ourselves, of relatively unspecified and uninvolved lookers-on. What they have witnessed appears to them as the metamorphosis of a fiction to a reality (which is, of course, exactly how it has been presented to us), "so like an old tale that the verity of it is in strong suspicion" (V.ii.28–29), "an old tale still, which will have matter to rehearse, though credit be asleep and not an ear open" (62–64). The problem which they have implicitly encountered in their own responses to this transmutation of an old tale to a verity is that with which Leontes has wrestled throughout the play and come to grips successfully through Camillo's drama: the problem of credit, or belief—unreserved, uncompromising belief in the natural order of love and the potential regeneration, through art, of the world to a state of harmony with that order. However, the very terms with which they describe what they have observed indicate that they have already opted to accept and credit this dissolution of the boundary between art and reality. Not only do they describe the kind of "wonder" (23) usually confined to the province of "ballad-makers" (24) as "broken out" (24) in the world, but they see the world itself increasingly as a work of art. The ideal indivisibility of art from life, the impossibility of which Shakespeare's Chorus earlier lamented in *Henry V,*

> A kingdom for a stage, princes to act
> And monarchs to behold the swelling scene
> (Prologue, 3–4),

is specifically celebrated by the Gentlemen of *The Winter's Tale:*

> The dignity of this act was worth the audience of kings and princes; for by such was it acted.
>
> (V.ii.79–80)

These uninvolved spectators, then, choose to credit the truth of that to which they have been audience, thus duplicating Leontes' act of belief and universalizing its significance by turning a new and believing perspective on their world at large: "Every wink of an eye, some new grace will be born" (110–111). Unmistakably, Shakespeare is suggesting that our own response be parallel to theirs, for we, too, have been mute onlookers to Camillo's artwork and Leontes' reaction. And just as the three Gentlemen have believed that an old tale can indeed come true, so we might choose to credit the verity, not only of Camillo's drama and its actualization in the play's world, but of the entire *Winter's Tale* containing these events and its potential actualization in our world. By adopting the Gentlemen's point of view, in other words, we will react to Shakespeare's artwork on the same terms as Leontes reacted to Camillo's—with a readiness to believe that it can be a reality and to participate in or at least actively approve its realization in our world.

This crucial parallel between ourselves in confrontation with *The Winter's Tale* and Leontes, along with the rest of the play-world's "audience members," in confrontation with Camillo's drama suggests further corollaries: we are being presented by Shakespeare with the dramatic image of an integrally ordered and harmonious world which, having fallen into chaos, can regenerate and restore itself to its unfallen state via the fictive arts of its inhabitants. If this image does not conform to the world as we know it, the chaos and moral dissonance of that world may have been due to our collective refusal until now, like Leontes in his original lapse of faith, to believe in the plausibility of a world such as Shakespeare shows us. And perhaps we are encountering in *The Winter's Tale* an artwork that, like Camillo's drama, might—through the catalyst of our belief and our willingness to act upon belief—break through the bounds of fiction and reform in its own image the world we inhabit, since that image only bodies forth our world's inherent and original truths.

Clearly, to an even greater extent than in the final movement of *King Lear,* the play is rapidly approaching a point of "recognition," as Northorp Frye defines the term, a point at which direct experience of the work comes into alignment with a critical view of it.[7] For we are experiencing not only the culmination of the play's events but an increasing, self-conscious awareness that we are responding to a work of art, and the nature of our response is coming to be of importance within the play itself. The climax of this recognition, as the climax of the play, occurs in Paulina's ultimate work of dramatic art, the unveiling and metamorphosis of Hermione's statue.

VI

Paulina has actually been the play's first character to apply dramatic artifice directly to circumstances of reality. After Leontes rejected as witchcraft her presentation of nature's non-illusory artifact in Perdita, Paulina undertook an illusory art of her own, convincing Leontes and the rest of the play-world's society, in her melodramatic tirade (III.ii.172–214) at the end of the trial scene, of Hermione's death. Her maintenance of this illusion for sixteen years has brought Leontes to an entire, repentant awareness of his sin of disbelief and a passionate eagerness to affirm and embrace any vestige of the natural order he originally denied—qualities that have rendered him so ideal an audience to Camillo's drama and the prime agent of its translation to reality. In the latter event, however, Paulina has witnessed a use of dramatic art on a broader scale than she has practiced it, for Camillo's device has accomplished far more than merely inducing, through illusion, a state of moral awareness in its audience. Rather, by presenting an overtly artificial image of the world as reconciled with its prelapsarian order, setting that image's ordered artifice against the world's chaotic reality, and thereby enlisting the active approval of its audience, Camillo's drama has overcome the barrier between itself and the real world and restored to the latter the essentials of its original order.

By observing this process, Paulina inherits the floral aesthetic which Camillo brought with him out of the green landscape of Bohemia: the principle that nature, the ultimate artist, can regain its rightful harmony with and control over the human world through the offices of a human work of art. And she puts this aesthetic directly into practice by employing an essentially dramatic medium to restore to the play-world's society Hermione, the original human representative of nature's inherent goodness and moral order. Just as the natural truth of Perdita's identity lay hidden for sixteen years until actualized in Camillo's drama, so Hermione has remained alive for sixteen years unknown to any but Paulina (whose comprehension of her own artwork's significance, in this respect, surpasses Camillo's); and Paulina accordingly undertakes to convey her back to the world at large through a theatrical event involving, like Camillo's, the metamorphosis of an artwork to a reality. Hermione is to be presented as a statue, an overtly artificial image, and—after a crucial dialogue between Paulina and her audience enlisting their entire faith and coactive approval—Hermione is to emerge from her artificial context and resume her place in the world.

The specific reasons for Paulina's unveiling Hermione through such an elaborately dramatic ritual rather than revealing her outright are twofold. Purely within the context of the play, Paulina intends to subject Leontes and the human world he represents to one final test of faith. Confronted with the unfeigned reality of Hermione and all the natural order for which she stood, Leontes rejected both through a diseased disbelief beyond logic. If Hermione is to resume her role as the human keystone of the play-world's restored order, then, Leontes must first guarantee the security of that order by an act of faith that is, like his lapse of faith, absolute and beyond the terms of logic: such a faith as will grant to an artwork, solely on the basis of the moral integrity which it images, the ability to transgress the norms of literal reality by becoming itself real. He has shown the potential for such faith in his confrontation with Camillo's image of natural order and his participation in its conversion to a reality. Here, as then, he will be confronted with an artwork imaging the essence of the order that defined his unfallen world; he will be invited to affirm his belief in that order and to substantiate that belief by actively endorsing the translation of the image to reality.

Paulina's *coup de théâtre*, however, will demand a more complete act of faith than Camillo's, which recommended itself to reality not on the grounds of its image's integrity alone, but partly on the level of practical possibility: as Florizel said, Perdita *would* be the daughter of a king once she were his wife (V.i.207–208). But in this case Leontes has no grounds for faith beyond the moral validity of the image itself, a statue, an entirely inanimate mimetic image. Beyond all logical limits of reality he must believe in and assist at the metamorphosis of this graven image of Hermione to Hermione herself. By such an uncompromising and absolute act of belief Leontes will fully negate his original disbelief in nature's order, proving himself and his world worthy to be shaped once again by nature's art. Indeed, as in Camillo's device, what he will unknowingly approve is in fact a work of nature's art: Hermione herself, whose face has been shaped and lined by a

> carver's excellence
> Which lets go by some sixteen years and makes her
> As she liv'd now.
>
> (V.iii.30–32)

The carver is not Julio Romano, but the natural condition of time itself; Paulina's arrangement of Hermione within this dramatic context is ultimately an art which itself is nature.

Yet there is another, broader purpose in this, the play's culminating event. Paulina's drama serves as a trial not only of Leontes' faith but of our own as well, since our response to the metamorphosis of Hermione's image will comprise our response to the combined experience of the play as a whole and will entail either our comprehension and approval or our rejection of the artistic self-definition which *The Winter's Tale* has set forth. For when we observe the event, the extent of our awareness as audience is no more than that of Leontes and all the other characters of his world, save the "artifact" herself and the artificer Paulina. Through the body of the play we have observed the entire evolution of Camillo's artwork—the circumstances that required it, the genesis of the aesthetic that informed it, the process of its preparation down to details of composition and costuming, and finally its successful performance—all from a point of view superior to those of its artist, its actors, and its onstage audience. We knew from the start that Perdita was the daughter of a king, that even her pastoral role-playing was an illusion that revealed a natural truth, an art that was itself nature; and we therefore knew better than Camillo how his drama could validly claim to become reality.[8] But as the scene in Paulina's gallery begins, we have no more knowledge than that Hermione has been dead for sixteen years. In fact, Antigonus' final speech (III.iii.15–58) has been calculated to confirm this belief. Our only preparation for the event comes in the previous scene from the three Gentlemen, whose dialogue has related to us the full blossoming of Camillo's endeavors and implied the parallel between the play-world community's relationship to Camillo's artwork and our own approach to Shakespeare's play. Immediately afterward, they inform us of another artwork, a statue of Hermione which they, along with all of the play's significant characters, are about to view (V.ii.93–103). And while this juxtaposition unavoidably suggests that we apply to Paulina's statue the same aesthetic criteria which we have seen applied to Camillo's drama, we have no logical reason to believe that what we are about to encounter is anything but an artificial image of Hermione. Our responses are in every way on a level with those of the characters whom Paulina ushers into her gallery. (This holds true whether or not we are already familiar with the play's ending. In terms of the play itself to this point we have no grounds for such superior knowledge, and if we are responding genuinely to the play, we will adopt the naive viewpoint Shakespeare affords us.)

Thus the moment when Paulina, in an overtly theatrical gesture, pulls aside the curtain and presents Hermione both to us and to the united community of the play-world resembles in an important way the final action of *King Lear*. In both cases the onstage and offstage communities are joined in a single audience focused on a single, static dramatic image comprehensive of all the play's experience; and in each case the presenter of that image demands that the audience recognize and achieve a communal response to it, sharing and affirming the import of the play as a whole. Just as Lear presented us with the dead Cordelia, Paulina presents us with the "dead" Hermione, both of them the embodiments of moral orders rooted in love and the bonds of kind, both of whose expulsions began their plays' respective cycles of chaos, and both of whose reappearances visually confirm the goodness of the orders they have represented. But while the moral essence of each play's consummate image is the same, the aesthetic and emotional reactions which they each invoke are not. As the worlds which *King Lear* and *The Winter's Tale* have sought to image emphasize contrary aspects of experience, so the ultimate communal responses demanded by each play (and thus the self-definition of each play in terms of its relationship to our world) are poles apart. *King Lear* presents us with a world that we have known in our darkest apprehensions of reality, demanding that we acknowledge those apprehensions and protest them, speaking what we feel, not what we ought to say. *The Winter's Tale* presents us with a world that few of us expect to experience outside the realm of art, demanding nevertheless that we affirm its plausibility and its accordance with our deepest hopes. In short, Lear calls on us to "look on" the corpse of Cordelia (*Lear*, V.iii.310) and "howl" (257), while Paulina invites us to "behold" the image of Hermione and "say 'tis well" (*W.T.*, V.iii.20). And this is only the first demand Paulina will make of us. For unlike Cordelia, Hermione may, with our assent, live again.

Leontes' initial reaction to the unveiled statue is exactly in accordance with the intent of Paulina's project:

> O, thus she stood,
> Even with such life of majesty, warm life,
> As now it coldly stands, when first I woo'd her!
> I am asham'd: does not the stone rebuke me
> For being more stone than it? O royal piece!
> There's magic in thy majesty, which has
> My evils conjur'd to remembrance
> (V.iii.34–40).

Purely as inanimate artifice, the "stone" evokes in him the response
of an emotional, almost sensuous remembrance—akin to the "looks"
he made at Perdita (V.i.227)—of the live Hermione and all the
goodness that lived with her, as well as a profound and final penitence
for his violation of that goodness. Perceiving this, Paulina takes care
first to establish her absolute control over the event as artist, referring
to the statue as "my poor image . . . for the stone is mine" (V.iii.57,
58); then, from this position of authority, she manipulates and
heightens the responses of her audience, particularly Leontes, to a
pitch of nearly inarticulate pain and longing. Repeatedly, almost cru-
elly, she suggests the desirability of the artwork's metamorphosis to a
living reality—"your fancy/May think anon it moves . . . . He'll think
anon it lives" (60–61, 70)—at the same time frustrating that desire by
reasserting the logical barrier between art and reality:

> The statue is but newly fix'd, the colour's
> Not dry
> .   .   .   .
> No longer shall you gaze on't
> .   .   .   .
> I'll draw the curtain
> .   .   .   .
> Shall I draw the curtain?
>   (47–48, 60, 68, 83)

Thus she brings her audience by degrees to a passionate readiness for
her project's culmination. Each time she threatens to draw the curtain
Leontes prevents her from doing so, consciously rejecting all worldly
norms of reality and declaring himself ready, on the basis of the image
she has wrought, to accept and believe anything that Paulina's art will
set forth:

> O sweet Paulina,
> Make me to think so [that Hermione lives] twenty
> years together!

No settled senses of the world can match
The pleasure of that madness.

(70–73)

Accordingly, Paulina makes her ultimate artistic claim: to convert her image to a reality; but she stresses as she does so the necessity of an absolute and unreserved faith on the part of all her audience. The success and validity of her art are now entirely conditional on the spectators' active belief:

> Either forbear,
> Quit presently the chapel, or resolve you
> For more amazement. If you can behold it,
> I'll make the statue move indeed; descend,
> And take you by the hand: but then you'll think
> (Which I protest against) I am assisted
> By wicked powers.
> *Leontes.*   What you can make her do,
> I am content to look on: what to speak,
> I am content to hear; for 'tis as easy
> To make her speak as move.
> *Paulina.*   It is requir'd
> You do awake your faith. Then all stand still:
> Or—those that think it is unlawful business
> I am about, let them depart.

(85–97)

Leontes formally reaffirms his preparedness to believe, reversing for the final time his original charge of witchcraft against Paulina. But Leontes' acquiescence alone is not enough at this point. That our own point of view is now not merely parallel to but fused with that of Leontes Paulina confirms by her twice-repeated invocation that all depart who cannot behold with full assent what is to occur. Clearly this demand reaches beyond the boundaries of the onstage world and addresses itself to all within the very "chapel" of the theatre itself. For the full denouement, not only of Paulina's project but of Shakespeare's play, can only be valid and meaningful through the belief and commitment of the entire audience, onstage and off. We are now directly confronted with the choice offered to Leontes. All who remain in the theatre after this point ritually repeat by their presence Leontes' declaration of active faith and, by the complete stillness which Paulina has called for, tacitly assist in the actualization of Hermione's image.

Thus all the play's levels of meaning—its definition of drama within its own fictive world and its self-definition as a work of art within our world—merge at this moment into the focus on a single dramatic image and hinge jointly on a single action. After a universal act of faith and assent by all spectators within and without the play, the play-world's ultimate work of art becomes its ultimate reality: when Paulina (like the Doctor in *Lear*) has called for music, the statue moves, descends, and, as Hermione, proffers her hand to her husband. Leontes, under Paulina's direction, leaves his position as a member of the audience, steps into her drama, and takes an active part as Hermione's lover by touching and embracing her. Art and reality are thereby equipoised and indistinguishable, the barrier between them dissolved. Leontes and Hermione become at once a dramatic image, observed and commented upon by an audience ("She embraces him!/ She hangs about his neck!" [111–112]), of the natural order that originally defined their world, and the real evidence of that order's consummate restoration to the world. Now, as at the play's start, the data of reality conform entirely to the perfect order of art, for man's world is once again aligned with nature's law and process; and nature, the ultimate artist, shapes an entirely ordered world through its dynamic of love and generation.

The fictive human arts that have effected this restoration by recreating human faith are now, therefore, as unnecessary as they were at the play's outset, since reality itself is an artwork of unsurpassable order. Accordingly, Paulina gradually abdicates her authority, deprecating what she has accomplished, ironically, as an incredible "old tale" (117); like Camillo's artwork, her impossible fiction has served

its highest purpose by becoming literal fact. She then attempts to
withdraw from the world altogether:

> I, an old turtle,
> Will wing me to some wither'd bough, and there
> My mate (that's never to be found again)
> Lament, till I am lost.
>
> (132–135)

But this must not be so; an unpaired turtle, young or old, is expressly
contrary to the play-world's restored natural order, under which, as
Florizel has said, "Turtles pair/That never mean to part"
(IV.iv.154–155). Leontes, now rightfully king over a harmonious
"world ransom'd," acts as nature's spokesman: "Thou shouldst a
husband take by my consent,/As I by thine a wife" (V.iii.136–137). If
the god Apollo himself is subject to the imperatives of the natural
order over which he presides, it is even more appropriate that Paulina
and Camillo take their places together in the harmonious world order
whose ransom their arts have jointly engineered.[9]

VII

Soon afterwards, with an almost jarring swiftness, all the members of
the onstage community "hastily lead away" (155), sweeping offstage
and taking with them all vestiges of the entirely ordered world they
now inhabit. We are left once again in our own world, and the image
stamped in our memories—Shakespeare's created artifact—is of a
world that is far from the one we know. Even before its abrupt vanish-
ing, Shakespeare stresses the gap between his world-image and our
world through Leontes' command that "Each one demand, and answer
to his part/Perform'd in this wide gap of time" (153–154). The theatrical metaphor reminds us both that all the events we have witnessed
have ultimately been a mimetic performance by actors and that the

world within *The Winter's Tale* is—at the play's conclusion as at its beginning—governed, unlike our own, by an order so complete as to admit of no distinction between art and reality.

Shakespeare thus specifically distinguishes between the art of his play and the reality of our experience—just as Camillo and Paulina stressed to Leontes the artificiality of their images of the unlikely and the impossible—in order that we may fully understand the relationship his artwork has defined between itself and us, the potentially vital function it has claimed in our world, and the pivotal responsibility it has placed on us. We have, in *The Winter's Tale*, witnessed the fall and regeneration of a cosmically ordered world through the lapse and restoration of its inhabitants' faith in its essential goodness. That restoration has been accomplished by two human works of dramatic art, each of which has imaged in its own way the play-world's original order, pointed out the gap between that image and the world's reality, and demanded from its audience the uncompromising and active faith required to make its image become a reality. In each case, the active, believing response of the audience has brought about a miraculous reordering of the play-world, manifested as the transformation of each image to a literal truth. In Camillo's drama we witnessed a full dramatic exposition of this process from a superior point of view. Paulina's drama then involved us in the theatrical moment of her image's metamorphosis, leading us through a ritual imitation of Leontes' active faith and thus providing us with a paradigm of response to the play as a whole.

Now, then, as Shakespeare offers, like Paulina, to draw the curtain on his own image, we are left with an avenue of response clearly defined for us by the play itself. We can, like Leontes, refuse to allow a curtain between our world and Shakespeare's image of a world, assailing the boundary between his art and our reality by awakening and acting upon our faith. We must consciously choose to afford Shakespeare's created world—beyond all the limitations dictated by empirical logic and the "settled senses of the world"—the degree of belief due to a potential reality, actively seeking in our own world the inherent goodness and moral order we have encountered in Shakespeare's art. Even as Perdita's royal identity and Hermione's life were brought to light through theatrical events, a universal act of faith such as the play now demands from us might uncover, as an enduring but concealed truth of our own existences, that same vital scheme of order which informs Shakespeare's world-image. Such are the final claims of the aggressive artistic manifesto that is *The Winter's Tale*.

Chapter Four

THIS ROUGH MAGIC:
"THE TEMPEST"

I

In the past two chapters we have seen how, in both *King Lear* and *The Winter's Tale*, Shakespeare has explored the problems and potentialities of his art in ways that are strongly parallel. Each play contains a number of sustained attempts by certain of its characters to confront or reorder the circumstances of the play's world through actions which are inherently exercises of dramatic art; and each play has shaped, through the ultimate successes or failures of those attempts, a definition of its own art in relation to our world and ourselves, thus presenting us with an aesthetic and moral means of apprehending our own experience.

However, the very closeness of this parallel accentuates the polarity of the views which the two plays present us of the world and of art as a means of dealing with the world. In *King Lear* Edgar creates a dramatic illusion of a morally and metaphysically ordered universe which is invalidated by the disorder of the play's real world. Accordingly, an alternative aesthetic is devised by Lear and confirmed in the art of the play itself by which the dramatic artwork can, through recognizing and reflecting the worldly chaos it cannot control, confront that chaos with an image of moral order that will endure in spite of it. In *The Winter's Tale*, on the contrary, Camillo and Paulina meet the disorder of their world, like Edgar, with dramatic fictions of an entirely harmonious world order, and their attempts are met with complete success. The natural moral order which their art images uncovers and activates a corresponding order that persists beneath the surface disorder of their world, and in the ensuing regeneration of that world to its original state their artworks not only control and alter but literally become reality. This, it is implied, is the potential role of the play's art in our world.

I should re-emphasize at this point that I am not presenting these opposed aesthetic views as two separate stages of Shakespeare's attitude toward his art and his world, but rather as the antinomial poles of a single artistic and moral vision. Besides the similar means by which each play defines itself artistically and the fact that both are written within the last six years of the dramatist's career, other aspects indicate an organic unity of vision encompassing the two works. Foremost is the concept of a moral order rooted in human love that emerges through both plays, informing the success of art within each play's world and providing the dramatic essence of the order which each play's art ultimately offers to communicate into our world. Since the plays present opposing perspectives on experience, the central imperative of that moral order is revealed in opposite ways. Lear discovers it in the depths of his suffering as the only human means of order available to set against the overwhelming tendency to disorder in human and non-human nature, while in *The Winter's Tale* the imperative to love is everywhere apparent as the key principle of an ordered continuum inherent in man and nature alike. But the same Shakespearean humanism—the same morality centered in recognition of, adherence to, and responsibility for one's kind—is constant throughout, even though projected in each play through antithetical modes of apprehension that correspond, respectively, to the tragic and comic phases of our experience.

In spite of this common moral vision, however, the fact remains that each play images a world and projects an aesthetic approach to that world which are in marked contrast to those of the other play; and it is clear that if, as I submit, Shakespeare simultaneously entertained the perspectives offered by both plays, he entertained them in a kind of ongoing dialectic that must, as he approached the end of his career, have called for some attempt at resolution. It is with these considerations in mind that we shall turn to a discussion of *The Tempest,* for in this play elements corresponding to the artistic and moral perspectives of both *King Lear* and *The Winter's Tale* are brought into play with one another in a single created world that is, to a certain extent, a composit of the other two plays. The result is a dramatic actualization of the dialectic we have traced through our juxtaposition of the earlier two plays, as well as a consummate expression of the moral order set forth by both. In this chapter, then, we will not only discuss, quite on their own terms, the perspectives of artistry that *The Tempest* bodies forth and applies to a definition of its own art, but as well view the play as the central panel in a dramatic triptych of Shakespeare's artistic self-consciousness.

II

Whether or not *The Tempest* was chronologically the last of Shakespeare's plays is a debatable and ultimately an irrelevant question. Nevertheless, there is an unmistakable sense of finality permeating the work. Themes and their variations that have appeared throughout the Shakespeare canon seem to draw together here. The characters include a hero more sinned against than sinning, a pair of young and innocent lovers, a guilt-ridden king, a faithful old councillor, a machiavellian usurper, a swaggering braggart, and a fool—all central character types of the tragedies, histories, and comedies, recapitulated and condensed in this most compact and precisely constructed of Shakespeare's plays.

More specifically, *The Tempest* deals centrally with ideas and concepts of art to a far greater extent than any of the plays before it.

All its events and circumstances are either the direct result or the consequence of Prospero's "Art." Here, for the first and last time in the canon, the artist is hero and protagonist, and his principal meditations, decisions, and actions are all couched in terms of his art. On the most immediate level, that art is presented as the skill of a formidable magician—an apparent demiurge, in effect, since he seems to control and order all the elements to the extent of raising a storm that splits a vessel and shipwrecks its passengers without "so much perdition as an hair/Betid" (I.ii.30–31) [1] to them or to the ship itself. Miranda associates his abilities with a "god of power" (10), and indeed his "so potent Art" (V.i.50) seems almost blasphemously close to godhead when he recalls rifting "Jove's stout oak/ With his own bolt" (45–46) and even raising the dead. Yet these are not powers naturally accruing to him; they were gained by years of seclusion and study (which cost him his dukedom), and they are embodied not in Prospero himself but in such objects as his books, his staff, and his magic garment. Without his books, says Caliban, "He's but a sot, as I am" (III.ii.91). Prospero himself perceives this separation of his artistic function from his identity as a man to the extent that he can, in putting off his garment, say, "Lie there, my Art" (I.ii.25).

Moreover, Prospero's magic lies not so much in a direct power over nature itself as in a masterful ability to imitate nature, to create and project mimetic images which can, in their fictive perfection, rival reality. Even the storm was a "spectacle" (I.ii.26): it was "Perform'd to point" (194) by Ariel, and all its lightnings and thunderclaps were in fact only semblances, as they did no harm. (One is reminded of Yeats' ultimate image of art in "Byzantium": "An agony of flame that cannot singe a sleeve.")[2] His subject spirits are never what they seem but continually assume roles and guises. Ariel plays a sea-nymph and a harpy, and his lesser cohorts appear variously in a number of spectacles and "urchin-shows" (II.ii.5) as apes, hedgehogs, adders, hunting dogs, and even goddesses. Ariel, in fact, offers Prospero the services of himself and "all his quality" (I.ii.193), and we recall that

contemporary actors referred to their profession as "the Quality." [3]
Prospero's remarks, after the banquet has been removed from before
the Court party, are the critical compliments of a director or actor-
manager congratulating his performers on a job well done:

> Bravely the figure of this Harpy hast thou
> Perform'd, my Ariel; a grace it had devouring:
> Of my instruction hast thou nothing bated,
> In what thou hadst to say: so, with good life
> And observation strange, my meaner ministers
> Their several kinds have done.
>
> (III.iii.83–88)

Finally, the masque presented in the fourth act is an overtly theatrical
event. Prospero's art, then, is a specifically dramatic art. Here, moreover, we are not witnessing, as in the previous two plays we have
studied, the gradual discovery and genesis of an art that defines itself
by degrees as drama. Prospero's powers as a dramatic artist confront
us in their full flower, a *fait accompli,* at the play's start. The first
image to meet our eyes, in fact, is not a natural phenomenon but, as
the following scene specifies, a mimetic show devised by Prospero and
performed by Ariel.

We are thus witnessing the powers of dramatic art at their fullest
possible potency—indeed, beyond the limits of what we normally
define as possible. In metaphorizing Prospero's artistry as magic,
Shakespeare is doing more than drawing on a subject of contemporary
interest. Northrop Frye has pointed out that magic, in its primary
form, involves a series of ritual, imitative acts accompanied by the in-
tonation of a myth or story which are intended to affect the order of
nature; thus water is poured on the ground, while an appropriate myth
is narrated, to cause rain. Drama begins in the renunciation of such an
end (or at least the recognition that it cannot be achieved), as the ritual
comes to be performed primarily for the sake of representing the myth
rather than controlling nature. But the impulse toward the former

goal—control of reality though imitation—remains submerged in the dynamics of the art.[4] We have seen how Shakespeare drew on this complex of associations in *As You Like It* by metaphorizing Rosalind's dramatic art and that of the play itself as magic, and how dramatic art within *The Winter's Tale,* as it showed itself able to control and alter the play-world's reality by making real the order which it imitated, came to be compared increasingly with magic, culminating in Leontes' pronouncement of Paulina's art as lawful magic. In Prospero's magic, then, Shakespeare is giving full expression to a theme close to the core of his artistic self-consciousness. We may well assume, therefore, that in *The Tempest,* to an even greater extent than in *King Lear* and *The Winter's Tale,* Shakespeare is working out through the body of the play a relationship between dramatic art and reality that figures an intended relationship between *The Tempest* and our world; and we shall trace that relationship through a close investigation of Prospero's artistry.

III

What, then, are the ends toward which Prospero employs his art; what, in other words, is the substance of the "project" to which he repeatedly refers? We can begin with his relationship to Caliban, who, while the most "monstrous" character of the play, is in effect the lowest common denominator of all its characters—indeed, of all humanity. He is the amoral, appetitive, suffering Self in all of us, ever in search of freedom to satisfy all its hungers—visceral, sexual, and emotional—and ever ready to follow any "god" who promises such freedom. Prospero's general method of dealing with this essence of fallen man is to check his degeneracy with verbal chastisement and physical pain—the "urchin-shows" (II.ii.5) of apes and adders—and to draw him up toward a state of fulfillment and moral regeneration. He teaches him how "To name the bigger light, and how the less"

(I.ii.337), and, through Miranda, how to speak. Moreover, besides specifically indicating the path to reformation, he shows him visions of some indistinct, heavenly ideal to spur him on further:

> and then, in dreaming,
> The clouds methought would open, and show riches
> Ready to drop upon me.[5]
>
> (III.ii.138–140)

Thus Prospero has employed his art to expose and chastise Caliban's faults, lead him to goodness, and show him visions of a future perfection. This morally didactic function is the basic pattern of almost all his artistic endeavors. He shipwrecks the Court party with the specific intention of subjecting Alonso, Antonio, and Sebastian to an ordeal of self-knowledge and purgation through the performance of his spirits, culminating in a show the climax of which is an invocation to "heart-sorrow/And a clear life ensuing" (III.iii.81–82). Ferdinand, too, undergoes a separate, punishing trial to rid him of his own "Caliban" qualities and to purify his love. Here again, the ordeal culminates in a mimetic vision of the ideal which Prospero intends him to assume: the masque of chastity.

Prospero's project, then, is no less than to purge the evil from all the inhabitants of his world and restore them to goodness. Like Edgar, Camillo, and Paulina, he undertakes to induce faith in a macrocosmic frame of moral order by creating and presenting fictive images of that order. Like Edgar, however, and unlike Camillo or Paulina, Prospero does not emphasize to his audience the fictive nature of his images but attempts to substitute them directly for reality. And Prospero is far more successful than Edgar at such manipulation of his audience's perceptions and actions. Thus his relationship to the rest of the play's characters—directing their lives, judging their flaws, and setting standards of goodness for them—is, again, close to one of godhead. Through Ariel he equates himself with the "Destiny,/ That hath to instrument this lower world/ And what is in't" (III.iii.53–55), and Ferdinand, in the presence of "So rare a wonder'd father and a wise"

(IV.i.123), thinks himself in Paradise. Such overt and implied resemblances have led some critics into mistaking Prospero for a figuration of God the Father. But it is precisely this assumption of godlike powers and responsibilities by one who is in no way superhuman that precipitates the central problem of the play. Prospero's artistic powers, being capable of great evil as well as great good, place him in a perilous position. To refer to the play's metaphorical plane of magic, the line between theurgy and necromancy could be thin at times, and the mage could easily cross it unawares; we need only remind ourselves that *prospero* is the Italian for *faustus*. And Prospero's art repeatedly evokes comparison with the magic of that other artist whose memory haunts the island: Sycorax, who employed her art not to order and improve nature but to deform it and torment its creatures. The negative possibilities of an art that can mislead and harm its audience constitute a serious spectre in this play. Unlike the world of *The Winter's Tale,* where all magic was lawful, Leontes' most deluded fears of wicked arts and witchery are a distinct possibility in the world of *The Tempest.*

In order to fulfill the responsibilities he has assumed, then—before he can presume to influence others with his art—it is imperative that Prospero himself have a comprehensive and flawless moral vision of his world. He must perceive not only what is evil in men and what, ideally, they should be, but also what men are and what relationship he, as a man, bears toward them. Our first insight into the moral vision on which his art is based emerges through his own narration (I.ii) of his first contact with evil in the world. We learn that, in the course of the "secret studies" (77) through which his art was acquired, he "grew stranger" (76) to his dukedom: rejected the everyday realities of statecraft for the ideal realm in his books. Like Lear, his sufferings began with a naive abdication of practical responsibility. But while Lear blinded himself to reality by a false concept of his universe, Prospero grew paradoxically isolated from reality through the pursuit of truth—truth in its abstract and ideal forms as couched in "the liberal Arts" (73). Being totally unaware or unsuspecting of the temptations of worldly power, he left the manage of his state to his brother, assuming that, since he reposed in Antonio an absolute love and a "confidence sans bound" (97)—the very qualities without which Leontes precipitated chaos in the world of *The Winter's Tale*— his love and confidence would naturally be returned. Instead, however, they "Awak'd an evil nature" (93), the throne was seized, and Prospero was cast away. His reaction to this eruption of evil is marked not simply by bitterness but by a pronounced incredulity "That a brother should/Be so perfidious!" (67–68). He was, and is still, unable to conceive of the contradiction between what a brother should be and what his brother was. Similarly, he cannot accept the fact that his own officers supported the usurper, that any evil could exist in the world as he knew it without being "new created/ . . . or chang'd . . ./ Or else new form'd" (81–83).

But primarily his amazement centers on the fact that his brother should have acted contrary to all logical and ideal norms of brotherhood—that his own kind could return hate where love was owed. The lapse of time has brought him no new understanding of this. He cannot even cope with its memory, and the increasing frustration of his failure to do so emerges in his irrational, peevish demands that his daughter attend him. He ignores Miranda's simple but profound bit of wisdom:

> I should sin
> To think but nobly of my grandmother:
> Good wombs have born bad sons.
> (118–120)

Such an acknowledgement of evil as part of the natural condition of man is unacceptable to Prospero. His years of seclusion in his library have instilled in him a moral perspective rooted not in the real world but in the ideals of his art. Significantly, he still prizes his volumes above his dukedom (68), and insists on judging the real world by their rigid moral absolutes. If his brother acted contrary to the ideal of a brother, then his brother was not a brother but some alien, inhuman thing of evil, to be dealt with as an enemy.

The dangerous short-sightedness of this view is self-evident, and it is further revealed in the history of his relationship to Caliban. Initially recognizing Caliban as a human creature, Prospero accepted him totally and afforded him all the "human care" (348) ideally due to a fellow being. He trusted him, like Antonio, sans bound, giving him the run of his cell and the unguarded company of his daughter, without a thought of any evil Caliban might do. Then, when the inevitable assault (Caliban being Caliban) occurred, Prospero, unable to connect such evil with any species but that of a devil-begotten, "poisonous slave" (321), an "earth" (316), a "filth" who deserved "stripes . . ., not kindness" (347), relegated Caliban to the status of an inhuman creature. As he overlooks Miranda's explanation of Antonio's evil—that good wombs have born bad sons—he misses the full implications of his own comparison of Ferdinand to Caliban (483): that Caliban's evil is an essentially human characteristic. There is a Caliban in the best of men. His presence and even his birthright must be recognized if he is to be effectively dealt with; for if left to run entirely at large he will inevitably perpetrate evil, and if disowned and repressed he will prove a greater threat by rebelling outright.

Of course, Prospero has not, at this point in the play, permanently disowned his affinity either to Antonio or Caliban. His ultimate intention, as his arrangement of the love between Ferdinand and Miranda indicates, is to reunite himself with all his enemies and so restore a harmony and order to his world in which, presumably, Antonio and Caliban will have their places. First, however, that world must be altered by his art to fit the letter of his moral vision, and the limits of that vision will not permit him to acknowledge as natural and human any being with the least taint of inherent evil. He will accept nothing short of a world where all brothers are entirely trustworthy and all monsters entirely harmless: a prospect similar in scope and impossibility to Gonzalo's island commonwealth (II.i.139–160). But Gonzalo never mistakes his own vision for more than a utopian reverie. Prospero, on the other hand, intends to eliminate, by force if necessary, all elements of humanity that will not conform to his vision. His project, then, is threatened with failure on two counts. Obviously his artistic ideal of a perfect world, given the morally imperfect nature of his fellow beings, can never be realized. Meanwhile, he is in constant danger of mistaking his own passionate resentment of the wrongs he has suffered for righteous indignation, thereby perverting his own goodness and wreaking havoc on those over whom he has power.

IV

Just as the artistic powers depicted in *The Tempest* are greater and more explicitly dramatic than in *King Lear* or *The Winter's Tale,* then, so the problem of the artist's own moral awareness and of its relevance to the success of his art is far more complex here than in either of the earlier plays. Edgar's error lay in his projecting as real a vision of a morally ordered cosmos; that vision was consequently shattered by the chaotic facts of a world that revealed itself in both its human and non-human natures to be inherently amoral and disordered. Accordingly, the art defined by the play itself had to acknowledge the existential disorder it was unable to control before imaging a moral order that might endure. In contrast, the artists of *The Winter's Tale* inhabited a fallen but inherently ordered and regenerative world, one in which human evil was an hysterical aberration from a morally harmonious norm. Camillo and Paulina had only to create living images of that omnipresent, natural morality and induce in their audiences a faith that there need be no division between the order of their artworks and the reality of the world, and their fictive visions graduated to realities. The world of *The Tempest,* however, contains ample elements of both plays' world-images: the inherent order of *The Winter's Tale* and the inherent disorder of *King Lear.* On one extreme of the play's human spectrum are Ferdinand and Miranda, limitlessly perfectable creatures whose nature is ideally apt to nurture and whose most instinctive impulses are, if anything, more virtuous than those of Florizel and Perdita. On the other extreme are Caliban—an image of natural man far darker than Poor Tom, being not only a poor, bare, forked animal but a dangerous one as well—and Antonio, who, if he is less attractive than Edmund, is fully his equal in instinctive villainy and remorseless machiavellianism. Between these extremes, moreover, are such morally ambivalent characters as Alonso and Sebastian, both of whom have shown themselves capable of evil and both of whom appear, in differing degrees, capable of redemption.

Thus if *King Lear* and *The Winter's Tale* deal with the tragic and comic extremes of experience, *The Tempest* sets out to encompass its full scale, imaging a world that is as threatening as it is hopeful, as potentially chaotic as it is potentially harmonious. It follows that Prospero's art must, in order to deal with such a world, encompass the artistries bodied forth in both the other plays. It must not only organize reality by creating images of moral order that will induce an answering response in the spectators, but it must also recognize and cope with that part of reality, and of its audience, which it cannot order or control. Necessarily, the moral vision that informs such an art must be of a scope unprecedented in either of the previous plays. We have seen that Prospero's vision initially lacks such scope, that he insists on superimposing a structure of preconceived absolutes upon his world, refusing to recognize any part of it that will not fit his structure. This serious defect in moral perspective creates an equally serious defect in his art, one that is most apparent in the dramatic spectacles climaxing the two principal phases of his intended project: the mortification and repentance of Alonso, Antonio, and Sebastian, and the matching of Ferdinand with Miranda.

The scenario of the ordeal Prospero has designed for the courtiers culminates in III.iii., as his spirits appear to them and perform to a solemn and strange music the masque-like action of setting a banquet before them. The purpose of this prelude is to instill belief in the spectators: to equip them with a readiness to perceive and credit the mirac-

ulous significance of what they are about to experience. And indeed
this end seems to be well accomplished. Sebastian proclaims:

> Now I will believe
> That there are unicorns; that in Arabia
> There is one tree, the phoenix throne, one phoenix
> At this hour reigning there.
> *Antonio.*   I'll believe both;
> And what does else want credit, come to me,
> And I'll be sworn 'tis true: travellers ne'er did lie,
> Though fools at home condemn 'em.
>   (III.iii.21–27)

But while in *The Winter's Tale* such affirmations of belief in the incredible on the part of Leontes and of the Gentlemen were clear evidence of moral regeneration, it will shortly become apparent that, at
least in the case of Sebastian and Antonio, much more is required of
Prospero's art to effect any significant change in his audience than
simply rendering them credulous.

The show proceeds with Ariel's entrance as a harpy and his climactic speech, which images to the three-man audience a clear scheme
of universal moral order, defining and judging them within it:

> You are three men of sin, whom Destiny—
> That hath to instrument this lower world
> And what is in't,—the never-surfeited sea
> Hath caus'd to belch up you; and on this island,
> Where man doth not inhabit,—you 'mongst men
> Being most unfit to live.
>   .   .   .   .
>   But remember,—
> For that's my business to you,—that you three
> From Milan did supplant good Prospero:
> Expos'd unto the sea, which hath requit it,
> Him and his innocent child: for which foul deed
> The powers, delaying, not forgetting, have
> Incens'd the seas and shores, yea, all the creatures,
> Against your peace. Thee of thy son, Alonso,
> They have bereft; and do pronounce by me

> Ling'ring perdition—worse than any death
> Can be at once—shall step by step attend
> You and your ways; whose wraths to guard you from,—
> Which here, in this most desolate isle, else falls
> Upon your heads,—is nothing but heart-sorrow
> And a clear life ensuing.
>
> (53–58, 68–82)

Like the climactic artworks presented to Leontes by Camillo and Paulina, this speech is calculated to evoke in the spectators remembrance of their original crimes and the conviction that they have offended against all the natural and supernatural powers of an ordered macrocosm, that the very seas and shores, incensed at their transgressions, are active agents in their punishment. And, again like the dramatic artworks of *The Winter's Tale,* Ariel's speech points out a course by which the spectators' crimes can be atoned for and their redemption attained. Prospero, however, does not present this vision as a created image but as a reality. Rather than, as Camillo and Paulina, offering his audience the choice of whether or not to actualize the moral order of the fiction confronting them by voluntarily acting in accordance with its imperative, he demands of them, directly in the name of the "powers" that govern the universe, "heart-sorrow/And a clear life ensuing," leaving them no alternative but "Ling'ring perdition," literally destruction and damnation. Thus the central, potentially tragic gap in Prospero's moral perspective emerges through the exercise of his art. He has, in a very real sense, confused his role as an artist with that of a god, forgetting his humanity in the process. In presuming to substitute his own sense of morality for cosmic law he has designated to himself a higher order of being and the right to reject, damn, and destroy his fellow man. It is in this vengeful aspect of his power that he exults far more than in the moral success of his artistry:

> My high charms work,
> And these mine enemies are all knit up
> In their distractions: they are now in my power,
> And in these fits I leave them . . .
>
> (88–91)

Significantly, Prospero exits immediately after this speech. So entirely confident is he of his dramatic vision's self-sufficient power over its audience that he does not stay to see its effect. We, however, do observe that effect, and it makes manifest to us an aesthetic flaw directly proportional to the artist's moral flaw. For Prospero has failed, in the isolated superiority of his perspective on humanity, to include or even recognize in his aesthetics the vital importance of his audience's voluntary response as a determining factor in the success or failure of his artwork. In point of fact, the harpy show affects only one of its spectators. Alonso fully accepts as truth the image he has witnessed, recognizing his conspiracy against Prospero as a sin against the entire order of creation and entering passionately into the way of remorse and mortification, the heart-sorrow, which Ariel's speech lays out for him:

> O it is monstrous, monstrous!
> Methought the billows spoke, and told me of it;
> The winds did sing it to me; and the thunder,
> That deep and dreadful organ-pipe, pronounc'd
> The name of Prosper: it did bass my trespass.
>
> (95–99)

Yet Alonso clearly has been predisposed to penitence before encountering Prospero's artwork, and he validates that artwork by the sympathetic response of his own conscience; indeed, it is likely that, had he known the vision confronting him to be a fiction, his response would, like that of Leontes, have been no different. Antonio and Sebastian, however, having already rejected all claims of the "deity" conscience (II.i.273), remain quite unaffected by the godlike demands which Prospero's spectacle makes of them. While they are fully convinced that the vision they have witnessed is real, they are in no way inclined to accept or participate in its moral order. They exit bragging wildly and essentially unchanged, rejecting the end of a clear life toward which Prospero's art has directed them; and they confound by their unrepentant malice the intended end of his artistic project: a universally ordered world entirely purged of evil. Prospero's drama, then, has here proved a partial failure; it has been discredited, like Edgar's, by the persistence of an unchanging reality which it can neither control nor come to grips with.

But Prospero has not remained to witness this gap in his project. He has, instead, gone to "visit / Young Ferdinand" (91–92), the one male character whose moral regeneration he has undertaken without the danger of giving way to motives of revenge, not only because Ferdinand has never wronged him, but also because he comes closest, along with Miranda, to fulfilling Prospero's standard of human goodness, thus affording ideal matter for his artistry. Prospero's management of the match between Ferdinand and Miranda relies, like the rest of his project, on key exercises of dramatic art, beginning with the carefully orchestrated meeting of the two in I.ii. Here the audience, those who are to be chiefly edified by the artwork, are significantly its chief actors as well. Ferdinand, led by Ariel's music, enters convinced that he is encountering some divine force moving through nature: "This is no mortal business, nor no sound / That the earth owes" (I.ii.409–410). Just as the court party are, by Ariel's performance, persuaded that the very seas and shores have condemned their sin, so Ferdinand believes what Ariel's songs tell him: that the "yellow sands" (377) and "wild waves" (380) bid him to join in a dance, a prearranged pattern that will lead to possibilities "rich and strange" (404). Thus he, too, is brought into a state of belief, of preparedness to apprehend some miraculous experience ordained for him by a providential, divinely organized nature; and his expectations are rewarded by the sudden appearance of Miranda, a natural "wonder" (429). They love at first sight, of course, but Prospero's art has wrought the experience of their love into a fine state of perfection and potentiality. They approach one another not only out of physical and emotional passion, but with reverence, awe, and the sense of a sacred significance in their actions. Prospero has readied Ferdinand to believe Miranda a "goddess" (424), and she, in turn, at first regards Ferdinand as "A thing divine" (421). Subsequently, as they adjust to the fact of one another's humanity, their love remains infused with a sacramental conviction of each other's essential divinity, and they enter willingly into the perfecting ordeal—for Ferdinand of service and for Miranda of compassion—which Prospero has laid out for them.

Under Prospero's direction, the courtship thus proceeds flawlessly and culminates with the lovers' formal betrothal in IV.i., the first concrete realization of the moral order Prospero intends to impose on his world. Here, presumably, the practice of his artistry and the validity of his ambition to reform the world in the exact image of his art should find their most substantial justifications. Yet in spite of all that he has accomplished, Prospero has overlooked in this phase of his project the same vital aesthetic factor he missed in not remaining to observe the effect of Ariel's performance on the court party: that his art alone, in all its sophistication and mastery, is incapable of affecting reality without a sympathetic, voluntary response from his audience. The innate goodness of the lovers themselves, as much as the skill of Prospero's art, has been responsible for the harmony and moral perfection of their union. As in the case of Alonso, the artificial vision of order which Prospero has shown them has been ratified only by their willing impulse to participate in such an order. However, by his excessively repeated (and, in performance, invariably comic) warnings to the lovers not to "give dalliance / Too much the rein" (IV.i.51–52), Prospero reveals his blindness to this fact; he can see their remarkable goodness only in terms of a code which he has imposed upon them and will subsequently impose upon his world. All, he conceives, has been and will be accomplished through the singular virtuosity of his art.

Prospero now celebrates that virtuosity in an elaborately dramatic presentation which, besides depicting the virtue of chastity he wishes to impress on Ferdinand and Miranda, constitutes an ultimate mimetic image of the perfect world he means to forge through his art. The masque, then, is the keystone of Prospero's artistry as it has been practiced so far in the play. As such, it is worth close consideration, for in both its artistic fabric and its final results the central aesthetic flaw of its creator's art and the moral blindness from which that flaw stems are clearly betrayed, this time becoming evident to Prospero himself and precipitating the play's central crisis. The show centers on Ceres, Juno, and Iris: goddesses, respectively, of the earth, the sky, and the rainbow that binds them together. They are the anthropomorphic embodiments of a nature that, like the elements Ariel has variously impersonated, substantiates and rewards the human values of Prospero's moral system. Theirs is a world from which all that is less than flawless, let alone evil, is rigidly exorcised. Yet the goddesses are being played by spirits like Ariel who are, in fact, elemental creatures of nature—the real nature surrounding Prospero—and they are compelled, possibly against their wills, to enact a natural order which is not their own, but Prospero's "pathetic fallacy." [6]

The chief details in Iris' opening description of the masque's landscape include "cold nymphs," "dismissed" and "lass-lorn" bachelors, vineyards which bear no fruit but are "pole-clipt," and a "sea-marge" that is "sterile and rocky-hard" (IV.i.60–70). This is a world not simply ordered and controlled but pruned and gelded of all that is spontaneous and primal, leaving only that which is cold, hard, and sterile. The culminating dance of nymphs and reapers brings to mind the sheepshearing scene of *The Winter's Tale* (IV.iv). There, however, the earthy, mildly ribald merriment of the Clown and his two girl-friends, along with a dance of satyrs, rounded out the human contours of Shakespeare's pastoral vision. But none dance in Prospero's pastorale that are not "properly habited" (IV.i.138: stage direction). Obviously, this vision fragments and distorts the realities of human experience. Venus and Cupid have been denied their rightful place in the pantheon, and the generative, sexual impulse they represent is strictly expelled from the world of the masque (86–101). Under such circumstances, the goddesses' invocations of "Earth's increase" and "foison plenty" (110) seem as unlikely as that "Nature should bring forth, / Of it own kind, all foison, all abundance" (II.i.158–159) on Gonzalo's island. There is no fertility or natural regeneration where the nymphs are cold and the bachelors lass-lorn. Ceres' "rich leas" are nullified by her pole-clipped vineyard and sterile sea-marge. Like Gonzalo's plantation, the "latter end" of Prospero's commonwealth "forgets the beginning" (II.i.153–154).

Shakespeare calculates the entire masque, then, to strike us as overtly artificial and unconvincing: a "vanity" (IV.i.41) of Prospero's art in a far more serious sense than Prospero himself means the term. Because his moral system ignores and is clearly at odds with a large sector of human reality, the artistic embodiment of that system fails to establish a viable connection with reality. Not that the specific ideal set forth in the masque, premarital chastity, is meant in itself to appear fallacious, but Prospero has set himself a greater goal than the depiction of an ideal; he means his art to encompass and directly influence reality. In his remarks to Ferdinand and Miranda (13–23) he has drawn no distinction between the cosmic scheme of the masque's world and that of the world outside it. On these terms, as a comprehensive image of the real world, the masque is bound to fail. Since it ignores the realities of earthly existence, it is incapable, as art, of comprehending or coping with the disorder of that existence, in particular the innate propensity for evil in human kind. No audience of less than the moral caliber and pliant obedience of Ferdinand and Miranda is likely to validate the masque's moral order by making it their own. The events of the play rapidly make this as clear to Prospero as it is to us. The wide disparity between the play-world of his art and the real world he inhabits is immediately revealed by an abrupt intrusion of extratheatrical reality. Just as Edgar's unreal dramatic image of a beneficently ordered universe was interrupted and upset by Lear's mad entrance and agonized truth-telling, so the morally precise nature of Ceres, Juno, and Iris is belied by the approach of three true naturals, Caliban, Stephano, and Trinculo, bent on rape and murder. The masque cannot co-exist with this sudden revelation, but "heavily" vanishes "to a strange, hollow, and confused noise" (IV.i.138: stage direction). Patently, the product of Prospero's art, having failed to acknowledge or come to terms with the reality of things as they are, cannot endure in the presence of that reality.

V

The failure implied in this premature termination of the masque is painfully evident to Prospero, who addresses Ferdinand in what amounts to an epilogue:

> Our revels now are ended. These our actors,
> As I foretold you, were all spirits, and
> Are melted into air, into thin air:
> And, like the baseless fabric of this vision,
> The cloud-capp'd towers, the gorgeous palaces,
> The solemn temples, the great globe itself,
> Yea, all which it inherit, shall dissolve,
> And, like this insubstantial pageant faded,
> Leave not a rack behind. We are such stuff
> As dreams are made on; and our little life
> Is rounded with a sleep.
>
> (148–158)

Unfortunately, this passage often has been misinterpreted as the elegiac central statement of *The Tempest*. In fact, it amounts to a bitter testament of nihilistic despair on Prospero's part, antithetical to the sense of affirmation the play will ultimately achieve. Shakespeare carefully reenforces this sense by specifying, through the observations of Ferdinand and Miranda, that Prospero speaks in "passion" (143), "touch'd with anger," and "distemper'd" (145); and Prospero himself recognizes that his "old brain is troubled" (159). The speech begins, as do Shakespeare's other epilogues (and as the epilogue of *The Tempest* will not), by acknowledging the dispersion of the masque's world-image; it is an "insubstantial pageant" with a "baseless fabric." But Prospero goes on to imply that as his artwork has proved baseless, so any attempt to order reality through art must ultimately fail, since reality itself is only a fading illusion. Thus, while he recognizes the failure of his art, he has not yet discovered the cause of this failure: the flawed moral perspective on which his art is based.

His vision is still as disastrously shortsighted as it was in his initial confrontations with Antonio and Caliban. Since reality will not conform to his concept of reality, he assumes that reality itself is unreal, that all the world and all humanity amount to no more than a flawed image that will fade into ultimate sleep—ultimate nothingness.

Retaining his misconception of himself as god rather than man, he assumes the right to condemn as unregenerate and destroy all that will not fit his moral code:

> A devil, a born devil, on whose nature
> Nurture can never stick; on whom my pains,
> Humanely taken, all, all lost, quite lost;
> .   .   .   .
>   I will plague them all,
>   Even to roaring.
>   (IV.i.188–190, 192–193)

Caliban is not a devil—thoroughly evil and unredeemable—but a type of humanity.[7] Prospero has earlier denied the humanity of the court party in the same way, calling them "worse than devils" (III.iii.36), and it is no coincidence that Stephano and Trinculo initially revealed their distorted perceptions by mistaking each other for devils (II.ii.90, 99). Prospero is committing the same error in a far graver sense; despairing in the nurture of Caliban, he despairs of the redemption of the low nature in all men and of his responsibility, as an artist, in the process of that redemption. Turning from despair to rage, he resolves to "plague them all," to strike out at all those (not only Caliban, Stephano, and Trinculo but very likely their three counterparts in the court party as well) whose evil qualities have frustrated him. As he summons hounds named "Fury" and "Tyrant" (IV.i.257), revelling in the pain of the clowns and exulting in the fact that "At this hour/Lies at my mercy all mine enemies," (262–263) his spirits become his "goblins" (258). Prospero has effectually abandoned the use of his art as a means of reforming his world, threatening instead to become a satanic personification of revenge. Tragic chaos impends.

Disaster is averted, however, by the action of Ariel, who intervenes as an advocate on behalf of Prospero's own "nobler reason" (V.i.26). The climactic crisis of the play passes in less than fifteen lines, as Prospero undergoes a brief but intensely meaningful *psychomachia*. Having described the whereabouts and miseries of the court party (and it was after a similar description of Caliban and his confederates that Prospero called up Fury and Tyrant), Ariel checks the momentum of Prospero's passion by charging him with the central moral obligation he has hitherto ignored in his artistry:

> Your charm so strongly works 'em,
> That if you now beheld them, your affections
> Would become tender.
> *Prospero.*   Dost thou think so, spirit?
> *Ariel.*   Mine would, sir, were I human.
> *Prospero.*   And mine shall.
>
>   (17–20)

Good or evil, flawed or perfect, they are human—as he is—and on this basis alone he is bound to commiserate with them, to forgive them, and ultimately to accept them:

> Hast thou, which art but air, a touch, a feeling
> Of their afflictions, and shall not myself,
> One of their kind, that relish all as sharply
> Passion as they, be kindlier mov'd than thou art?
> Though with their high wrongs I am struck to th' quick,
> Yet with my nobler reason 'gainst my fury
> Do I take part: the rarer action is
> In virtue than in vengeance.
>
>   (21–28)

As an artist, he must limit his ends to the revelation of truth and self-knowledge; as a man, he can presume no further:

> They being penitent,
> The sole drift of my purpose doth extend

> Not a frown further. Go release them, Ariel:
> My charms I'll break, their senses I'll restore,
> And they shall be themselves.
>
> (28–32)

His moral vision is completed by the discovery and acceptance of this one truth: the overriding necessity for recognition and acceptance of all that is human—in short, for love. This has been the element missing in his artistry, the flaw that rendered the harpy-show and the masque of the goddesses inadequate. Only through unconditional forgiveness and acceptance of human nature, after all that can be done to reform it, can an art be capable of comprehending and dealing with the realities, good and evil, of the world. Prospero, then, finds himself as an artist as well as a man. What he rejects in the "elves of hills" speech (33–57) is not his art *in toto*, but his "rough magic" (50): that aspect of his art by which he presumed to rise to a Jove-like stature over other men, refusing to forgive them or accept their kinship as fellow beings until he had made them over in the image of his own moral perspective. In drowning his book he does away not with the essence of his art but with that same volume he has prized above his dukedom, above the society of his fellows: his blind absorption in the ideal to the exclusion of the real and the human. Far from the end of his artistic powers, this marks the point at which his art truly begins to function effectively.

The ultimate end of his artistic project, the restoration of order and harmony to the real world, starts to materialize as he frees and formally forgives each of his enemies. Not only does his art, like that of *King Lear,* acknowledge the disorder it cannot control, but the artist in this case pardons and embraces the human agents of that disorder. The simple act of forgiveness might seem too pat a solution of the play's central problem if its difficulty were not made absolutely clear. As Prospero's confrontation with the evil in human nature was first represented by his alienation from his brother, his acceptance of that nature is affirmed in Antonio's pardoning:

> Flesh and blood,
> You, brother mine,
>
> .   .   .
>
> I do forgive thee,
> Unnatural though thou art.
> (74–75, 78–79)

The words come haltingly. It is obvious enough that Antonio has not opted for "heart-sorrow and a clear life ensuing," that, given the chance, he will repeat his crimes. Prospero must force himself to forgive by sheer strength of will, repeating his pardon twice during the scene as if to convince himself; for he has undertaken an act of love more strenuous than those which ultimately faced either Lear or Leontes. It is not a Cordelia, a Perdita, or a Miranda whom he recognizes and accepts as "flesh and blood," but a creature of truly "unnatural" evil. Having done so, however, he can proceed toward the climax of his project by presenting his consummate dramatic artwork.

That artwork proves his most successful of the entire play, and in its success it illuminates the principal aesthetic corollary, the lack of which has disabled him until now, of his completed moral awareness. For Prospero, in his new recognition of his fellow man, has finally understood that the ultimate validation of his art, the metamorphosis of its fictive moral order to a worldly reality, can come about only through the spontaneous and authentic response of a conscious, freely choosing audience. By formally releasing the court party from his spell and thereby abandoning his manipulative power over them he has purposefully created such an audience, such a true theatrical community. Confronting that community—not invisibly now but as himself, the "sometime Milan" (86), one of their kind—he presents his last spectacle to them, not as a supernatural vision or a prodigy of the elements, but as no more and no less than what it actually is: his own work of art. Offering a "wonder" to "content" them (170), he draws aside the curtain to reveal Ferdinand and Miranda at play, a dramatic image that is, unlike any of his previous works, at once a product of Prospero's art and an entirely natural, flesh and blood reality.

Thus the main action of *The Tempest* culminates, as do those of *King Lear* and *The Winter's Tale*, in a presentation to the gathered, onstage community of a visual emblem charged with the cumulative significance of the play's moral order—one rooted in love—and in the community's manifest recognition of that emblem. But the scope of the communal recognition here is greater than in the other two plays. The community that viewed Lear and Cordelia and that which viewed the statue of Hermione had been purged of all unbelieving and unsympathetic spectators, the former by death and the latter by Paulina's specific edict that all who considered her business unlawful quit the chapel. Prospero, however, has forged a far broader community, one representative of all his kind, villains and skeptics included. Sebastian, in fact, has charged that "the devil speaks in him" (129), the very sort of accusation in the presence of which Paulina refused to work her art.

Notwithstanding, Prospero declines to limit his audience in any way; he is determined to present his last artwork to the whole community of his fellow beings, either to be validated or marred by their free choice of response. Therefore, the joyful approbation which it does elicit is of proportionally greater significance. Sebastian himself, who has least cause, in Machiavellian terms, to rejoice at what he sees, quite unexpectedly reverses his ground with the spontaneous exclamation, "A most high miracle!" (177). The image of the lovers has moved him far more than the terrors of the harpy-show, and Prospero's art may indeed have caused a most high miracle within Sebastian himself.

Prospero's final artistic endeavor, then, meets with full success. As the young couple emerge, like Hermione, from the static tableau in which they have been presented to take their places in the community, order radiates outward from Prospero's artwork into the world of the play. Prospero regains his dukedom, the reformed Alonso finds his son, and the perpetuation of harmony is insured by the bethrothal of the lovers. All these have found themselves through Prospero's art "When no man was his own" (213), and Prospero himself is no exception; his has been the last and greatest self-discovery. A wonder, akin to that shared by all characters at the conclusion of *The Winter's Tale,* now descends on all the community but Prospero. For him it is not a "brave new world" (183). He is aware that the preservation of order will continue to require the recognition of, the attendance to, and ultimately the forgiveness of evil; and he affirms this on a broadly representative scale by reacknowledging his responsibility for, and even kinship with Caliban: "this thing of darkness I/Acknowledge mine" (275–276). And even here, at the lowest level of human nature, forgiveness sparks hope as Caliban resolves to "be wise hereafter/And seek for grace" (294–295). Antonio, of course, remains ominously silent, but it is the very live presence of his unreformed evil that underlines the triumphant order which has been achieved in spite of it. By including Antonio in the onstage community at the moment of his ultimate artwork's unveiling, Prospero has forged an image of love's order that not only embodies the regenerative fulfillment and redemptive harmony that informed Hermione's live statue, but retains the indestructible endurance in the face of disorder that distinguished the death tableau of Lear and Cordelia.

VI

The success of Prospero's last dramatic artwork has thus effected a conclusive definition of art within the world of *The Tempest* that encompasses the concerns of the two other plays we have studied. And this in turn provides the basis for a definition of the art of the play itself in relation to our world, one that likewise incorporates both the optimistic possibilities of *The Winter's Tale* and the stringent realities of *King Lear.* This definition is not merely implied but formally presented, as Prospero speaks directly to us in one of the most remarkable and comprehensive extradramatic statements in the Shakespeare canon. The speech fits the genre of an epilogue, but within that genre it is highly unconventional. Nearly all other Shakespearean epilogues declare or assume the termination of the play-world, calling their audi-

ences back to an extratheatrical norm of reality and requesting applause.[8] This pattern is surprisingly consistent, whether couched in the
utilitarian prose of the Dancer in *2 Henry IV* or the finely wrought
verse of Puck. The most concise and representative example is the Epilogue of *All's Well That Ends Well,* spoken by the King:

> The King's a beggar, now the play is done.
> All is well ended if this suit be won,
> That you express content; which we will pay,
> With strife to please you, day exceeding day.
> Ours be your patience then, and yours our parts.
> Your gentle hands lend us, and take our hearts.

The first line dominates those that follow; it leaves no doubt that the
standards of identity and reality in the play-world have come to an end
and bear no relevance to the present situation. The speaker is no
longer the King but an actor. The play, its events, and its characters
are offered simply as "our parts," objects of artifice for the pleasure
and approval of the audience.

The Epilogue of *The Tempest,* however, specifically does away
with this conventional perspective, proposing rather to eliminate any
barrier between Prospero's world and ours:

> Now my charms are all o'erthrown
> And what strength I have's mine own,
> Which is most faint: now, 'tis true,
> I must be here confin'd by you,
> Or sent to Naples. Let me not,
> Since I have my dukedom got,
> And pardon'd the deceiver, dwell
> In this bare island by your spell;
> But release me from my bands
> With the help of your good hands:
> Gentle breath of yours my sails
> Must fill, or else my project fails,
> Which was to please. Now I want
> Spirits to enforce, Art to enchant;

> And my ending is despair,
> Unless I be reliev'd by prayer,
> Which pierces so, that it assaults
> Mercy itself, and frees all faults.
> As you from crimes would pardon'd be,
> Let your indulgence set me free.
>   (Epilogue, 1–20)

While the opening three lines lead us to expect a conventional declaration by an actor who is only an actor, the "charms" of his art "o'erthrown," such an expectation is then deliberately undercut; it is still Prospero who speaks—from the island, not from the stage—and the play has yet to reach a conclusion. Moreover, its final event, the impending return to Naples, is charged to us. It is our "spell" that holds him confined; our hands must release him and our "gentle breath" supply the "auspicious gales" which he has promised Alonso (V.i.314). In effect, we are invited to enter the play and assume a role as a moving force in its culmination. Nor is this simply a metaphoric request for applause; without such participation on our part, we are told, Prospero's "project fails"—that same project we have watched evolve through the play and gather to a head in the fifth act. An appeal for applause is thus delivered, but it is spoken from within the play. Rather than stepping out of his dramatic context to address us in our own sphere of reality, Prospero offers to bring us into the world of the play. Here and here alone in Shakespeare, far more explicitly than in *The Winter's Tale,* the play recognizes no terminal boundaries to its art, but rather moves to subsume the real, extratheatrical world of its spectators, to supplant our sense of reality with its own.

But this triumphant mergence of our world with that of the play is not stated as an accomplished fact. It is a possibility, along with the equally explicit possibility of the project's failure and the artist's "ending" of "despair." The outcome is directly contingent upon our own free choice at this point, and our choice must involve more than applause alone. Just as the harpy-show proved a partial failure by the moral indifference of the greater part of its audience, the masque of

the three goddesses was dispersed by the physical proximity of the
three rebels, and the success of Prospero's final spectacle lay in the
spontaneous recognition and acceptance of the majority of its spectators, so the ultimate ratification or invalidation of the vision which
Shakespeare has developed—for certainly Shakespeare speaks with
Prospero at this point—must come from us. The art of Shakespeare as
well as of Prospero will prove a vanity unless we affirm its validity by
sharing the moral discovery that informs it, participating in a cognate
act of the love and forgiveness which are the essence of that discovery. Therefore, Prospero places us in circumstances exactly parallel to
the moment of his own climactic decision, charging us with the same
responsibility. As Ariel reminded him that the courtiers were "Confin'd together" and could not budge "till your release" (V.i.7, 11), so
Prospero must be "confin'd" until we "release" him. As he has
"pardon'd the deceiver" we must set him free by our own "indulgence." In entering Shakespeare's created world, then, we must
not only embrace its inherent goodness and perfectibility as potential
realities in our own world but accept as well its inherently chaotic
aspects—the amoral appetitiveness of a Caliban, the cold malice of an
Antonio, and the presence of both in all men, Prospero included—as
inevitable traits of our own kind. If we pardon in Prospero what he has
pardoned in his fellows, we participate in the culmination of his project. If we choose to do otherwise, the ending is despair.

Thus Shakespeare, like Prospero, ultimately stakes the success or
failure of his art on the communal response of his audience, and the
response requested of us entails both an act of faith equivalent to that
required at the end of *The Winter's Tale* and a confrontation with reality in its way no less rigorous than that demanded at the end of *King
Lear*. It is an unprecedented request to make of an audience, one equal
in scope to the requirements which, through Prospero, Shakespeare
has set on his own art. But the conclusion of the Epilogue evinces a
similarly unprecedented confidence on Shakespeare's part in both his
art and our response to it. His use, in the last five lines, of such
overtly religious terms as "prayer," "Mercy," and "indulgence"

links his artistic vision with the orthodox principle of Christian charity, implying that if his audience can make his vision their own they will be participating in an act of prayer, bringing down mercy and redemption on both the pray-er and the prayed-for. By thus endowing the moral order of love which his play has set forth with the universal validity associated by his contemporary audience with the theological framework of their cosmos, Shakespeare affirms his faith that his project can be fulfilled: that his vision can pass beyond the created world of his play and merge with the world surrounding it. His ultimate definition of his own dramatic artistry—of its aims, problems, and possibilities in our world—thus culminates in the anticipation of a communal ceremony of affirmation, one in which playwright, actors, and audience can unite in a recognition, acceptance, and celebration of our shared humanity.

NOTES

CHAPTER ONE—INTRODUCTION

1. Jean Genet, *The Balcony*, trans. Bernard Frechtman (revised version, New York, 1966), pp. 95–96.

2. George Puttenham, *The Arte of English Poesie*, ed. Gladys Doidge Willcock and Alice Walker (Cambridge, 1936), p. 3.

3. Sir Philip Sidney, *The Defence of Poesie*, ed. Albert Feuillerat (Cambridge, 1923), pp. 7–8.

4. Also, the correspondence posited between the Maker's art and that of his creatures is reflected, in the plays we shall study, by the correspondence between the playwright's art and that of the characters he has created.

5. All Shakespearean line references except those from *King Lear, The Winter's Tale,* and *The Tempest* are to the text in *Shakespeare: The Complete Works,* ed. G. B. Harrison (New York, 1948).

6. Anne Righter, *Shakespeare and the Idea of the Play* (London, 1962).

7. Ibid., pp. 148–186.

CHAPTER TWO—NATURE'S ABOVE ART: *King Lear*

1. John Keats, "Sonnet: On Sitting Down To Read *King Lear* Once Again," in *Poetical Works,* ed. H. Buxton Forman (London, New York, Toronto, 1908), pp. 302–303.

2. All references from *King Lear* are to the text of the New Arden edition, ed. Kenneth Muir (London, 1963).

3. Samuel Johnson, *Rasselas, Poems and Prose,* ed. Bertrand H. Bronson (New York, 1958), p. 297.

4. *Five Restoration Adaptations of Shakespeare,* ed. Christopher Spencer (Urbana, 1965), pp. 201–274.

5. A. C. Bradley, *Shakespearean Tragedy* (Second Edition: London, 1905), p. 285.

6. O. J. Campbell, "The Salvation of Lear," *ELH,* XV (1948), 107.

7. Bradley, *Shakespearean Tragedy,* p. 291.

8. Paul N. Siegel, *Shakespearean Tragedy and the Elizabethan Compromise* (New York, 1957), pp. 185–186.

9. Jan Kott, *Shakespeare Our Contemporary* (New York, 1964), pp. 87–124.

10. The most celebrated is that directed by Peter Brook for the Royal Shakespeare Company in 1962. For critical discussions of this and other productions of the same bent, see V. A. Kolve, "The Modernity of Lear," *Pacific Coast Studies in Shakespeare,* ed. Waldo F. McNeir and Thelma N. Greenfield (University of Oregon, 1966), pp. 173–189; and Maynard Mack, *King Lear in Our Time* (University of California, 1965), pp. 28–41. Kolve points out quite aptly that the Kott-Brook approach seeks to curtail the play in order to fit our own era's view of things as much as did adaptations by Tate and the Augustan editors.

11. J. Stampfer, "The Catharsis of *King Lear,*" *Shakespeare Survey,* XIII (1960), 1–10.

12. I interpret "opposeless" to indicate that the Gods are too powerful for the living to oppose—not that the Gods *should* not be opposed, which would render the speech illogical. In opting for suicide, Gloucester is opposing the Gods in the only way he deems possible.

13. Indeed, his project is to have even graver results in the course of the play. The next time Edgar insists that his actions "sav'd" Gloucester "from despair," it will be by way of reporting Gloucester's death of a burst heart, "too weak the conflict to support" of Edgar's unmasking in reward for Gloucester's spiritual regeneration. Edgar himself will admit it a "fault" that he had not revealed himself earlier (V.iii.191–199). This is an understatement, for we know that at the moment Edgar resolved to "daub it further" (IV.i.51), Gloucester had expressed an overriding human desire, the satisfaction of which would far more effectively have saved him from despair:

> Oh! dear son Edgar,
> The food of thy abused father's wrath;
> Might I but live to see thee in my touch,
> I'd say I had eyes again.
>   (21–24)

Edgar, however, chose to retain his mask and act out his drama, trifling not only with despair but with human life itself.

14. Stampfer, "Catharsis of *King Lear,*" p. 4.

15. John Danby, *Shakespeare's Doctrine of Nature: A Study of King Lear* (London, 1949), p. 191.

16. Wallace Stevens, "The Idea of Order at Key West," *Poems,* ed. Samuel French Morse (New York, 1959), p. 56.

17. Sir Philip Sidney, *The Defence of Poesie,* ed. Albert Feuillerat (Cambridge, 1923), p. 8.

18. John Ruskin, *Works,* ed. 1903, XIV, 17. Quoted by Kenneth Muir in the New Arden edition of *King Lear* (p. 191*n.*)

19. *Cf.* George Puttenham, *The Arte of English Poesie,* ed. Gladys Doidge Willcock and Alice Walker (Cambridge, 1936), p. 303. Puttenham refers to the Physician (along with the Gardener—an interesting analogue to *The Winter's Tale*) as an example of the respect in which "arte is not only an aide and coadjutor to nature in all her actions, but an alterer of them, and in some sort a surmounter of her skill, so as by means of it her owne effects shall appeare more beautifull or straunge and miraculous, as in both cases before remembered."

20. Albert Camus, *The Rebel,* trans. Anthony Bower (Harmondsworth, Middlesex, 1962), p. 29.

21. Bradley, *Shakespearean Tragedy,* p. 291. Bradley's reading has its foundation, obviously, in Lear's particular reference to Cordelia's lips, recalling his earlier demand for a looking glass and his use of a feather, both to hold up to her lips as a test of whether or not she lives. I suggest that Lear is, by this reference, calling attention to the negative result of that test. He knows when one is dead and when one lives; she is indeed dead as earth, and Lear is demanding that we all confront that fact. Here, of course, as is often the case in Shakespeare's plays, the meaning of the speech must depend to a considerable extent on the actor's manner of inflection. Even so, S. F. Johnson has pointed out to me that—however Lear's attitude is interpreted—his reference to "her lips" relates to the persistent idea of the departure of the spirit of the dead through the mouth, as in countless paintings and emblems.

CHAPTER THREE—THE ART ITSELF IS NATURE: *The Winter's Tale*

1. E. M. W. Tillyard, *Shakespeare's Last Plays* (New York, 1938), pp. 84–85.

2. All references from *The Winter's Tale* are to the New Arden text, ed. J. H. P. Pafford (London, 1963).

3. John Anthony Williams, *The Natural Work of Art: The Experience of Romance in Shakespeare's Winter's Tale* (Cambridge, Massachusetts, 1967), p. 2; the quotation is adapted from Frank Kermode, ed., *The Tempest* by William Shakespeare (London, 1954), p. liv.

4. V. A. Kolve, "The Modernity of *Lear,*" *Pacific Coast Studies in Shakespeare,* ed. Waldo F. McNeir and Thelma N. Greenfield (University of Oregon, 1966), p. 175.

5. One of the more illuminating such studies that I have read is in Edward William Tayler's *Nature and Art in Renaissance Literature* (New York and London, 1964), pp. 121–141.

6. Anne Righter, *Shakespeare and the Idea of the Play* (London, 1962), p. 198.

7. Northrop Frye, *A Natural Perspective: The Development of Shakespearean Comedy and Romance* (New York and London, 1965), p. 9.

8. This bears out significantly Madeleine Doran's observation (*Endeavors of Art: A Study of Form in Elizabethan Drama* [Madison, 1963], p. 328) regarding Shakespeare's management of the romantic discovery as opposed to Fletcher's: that Shakespeare consistently provides us with a knowledge, unavailable to the play's characters, of the concealed identities at the heart of the plot's complications, thus affording us an ironic perspective on the action. Shakespeare's distinct departure from this technique in the discovery of Hermione, then, is all the more significant.

9. I have not mentioned the significance of Autolycus' action of luring the Clown and Shepherd aboard Florizel's ship, which has, of course, a decisive influence on the play's outcome by making Perdita's identification possible. But this does not, I think, contradict my overall reading of the play; for Autolycus, too, works his knaveries by an unmistakable (though much debased) kind of dramatic artifice. He is an infinite role-player and shape-changer, rarely appearing without an elaborate guise, and he attains all his ends—pickpocketing the Clown, selling his ballads, and bringing the Clown and Shepherd to Sicilia—through eliciting and manipulating the unreserved belief of his audiences. At the height of his powers he exclaims in theatrical jargon, "Sure the gods this year connive at us, and we may do any thing extempore" (IV.iv.676–677). In one sense this offers a parodic perspective on the efforts of Camillo and Paulina, since the faith which Autolycus instills is outright gullibility. But there is a deeper irony here, for in eliciting the entire belief of his last two victims he quite unwillingly brings them to happiness and prosperity, aiding unaware the regeneration of the play-world.

Autolycus also offers us a key to the assertive optimism of the play's world-image; for he is distinctly similar to Edmund in *King Lear*. Both are adept role-players and deceivers; both pursue entirely selfish, amoral ends with lustiness, appetite, and energy, sharing their escapades with the audience; and both identify themselves, at the outset, with the processes and prerogatives of nature (Autolycus' opening songs are as clear a manifesto as Edmund's first soliloquy). The ends they achieve, then, are a significant indication both of the respective kinds of nature on whose behalf they act and of the possibilities of dramatic artifice within those natures. Edmund's play-acting with Gloucester and Edgar helps bring down whatever structures of order remain after Lear's abdication, increasing the chaos that floods into the play's world, while the utmost of Autolycus' roguish deceptions only contribute to the overall harmonious order which nature is effecting through human works of art.

CHAPTER FOUR—THIS ROUGH MAGIC: *The Tempest*

1. All references from *The Tempest* are to the New Arden edition, ed. Frank Kermode (London, 1954).

2. W. B. Yeats, *The Collected Poems* (New York, 1956), p. 244.

3. Henry Chettle, for instance, in his *Kind-Harts Dream*, terms Shakespeare "exelent in the qualitie he professes" (quoted in E. K. Chambers, *William Shakespeare*, [Oxford, 1930] Vol. I, p. 58).

4. Frye, *A Natural Perspective* (New York and London, 1965), pp. 59–60.

5. Such visions are, of course, seen "in dreaming," but since Caliban has been put to sleep by "twangling instruments" and voices, it is reasonable to suppose that, like the sleeping courtiers in II.i., he is under the influence of Prospero.

6. Caliban claims that Prospero's spirits "all do hate him / As rootedly as I" (III.ii.92–93), and the fact that Ariel, the most faithful and loving of them, comes close to open rebellion in the first act, indicates that there is at least some truth to this.

7. Prospero, of course, claims that Caliban was "got by the devil himself" (I.ii.321), but there is no concrete proof of this. Caliban, who makes frequent references to his mother and her god, never mentions an infernal father. In any case, his qualities as a character are clearly not satanic but human. He is disposed toward evil, but only in the sense that man, at his worst, is so disposed. He never consciously chooses evil—as do Shakespeare's more authentic demi-devils, Iago and Richard of Gloucester—but constantly mistakes it for good: he sees Stephano as a god and anarchy as freedom.

8. There are nine epilogues in Shakespeare—eleven if we count Feste's last song in *Twelfth Night* and Armado's concluding lines, which may or may not be addressed to the audience, in *Love's Labor's Lost*. The rest are in *A Midsummer Night's Dream, 2 Henry IV, As You Like It, Henry V, Troilus and Cressida, All's Well That Ends Well, Pericles, The Tempest*, and *Henry VIII*. At the end of *Troilus and Cressida*, Pandarus assaults the barrier between the play-world and the real world, speaking directly to the pimps and prostitutes in the audience and bequeathing them his diseases. As in *The Tempest*, convention is overturned for a specific effect. The effect in this case, however, is only to impress the audience with the fact that forms of degeneracy exist in their world parallel to those depicted in the play. This is a comparison of the two worlds: not the complete interpenetration proposed in *The Tempest*.

INDEX